"The kingdom of God is cent[...] central in our theology. A clea[...] volume helps us both understa[...] the Bible through the vantage point of the kingdom of God."

Christopher W. Morgan, Dean and Professor of Theology, California Baptist University; editor, *The Kingdom of God* and *The Glory of God*; contributor, *Systematic Theology Study Bible*

"Patrick Schreiner's biblical theology of the kingdom of God is exactly what the church needs to help her pursue God's justice on earth: a lucid, precise, and concise book about the kingdom of God that's grounded in accessible biblical exegesis and provides keen theological insights, while keeping the cross of Jesus at the center of the analysis. Highly recommended!"

Jarvis J. Williams, Associate Professor of New Testament Interpretation, The Southern Baptist Theological Seminary

"Patrick Schreiner has given a wonderful gift to the church through this book on the kingdom of God. It's a creatively written and accessible entryway into this essential biblical theme. Schreiner honors the unified narrative shape of the Old and New Testaments, and he shows how every part of the Bible (including the Wisdom Literature!) contributes to the developing portrait of God's kingdom over creation and new creation. If you've ever struggled to understand this complex biblical theme or tried to communicate it to others, you've now found the place to start."

Tim Mackie, Cofounder, The Bible Project; Adjunct Professor of Biblical Literature, Western Seminary

"To say that the story of the Bible is the story of the King and his kingdom is one thing; to see it clearly and concisely demonstrated from every part of the Bible is another. I look forward to recommending this book to those who love and appreciate biblical theology as well as those who love Christ and the Bible but haven't yet understood how to see King Jesus throughout its entire story."

Nancy Guthrie, author, Seeing Jesus in the Old Testament Bible study series

"Patrick Schreiner beautifully traces the theme of God's kingdom through the entire Bible. The threads of his kingdom can be seen from Adam to Abraham, through Psalms and Isaiah, to Jesus and his church, and finally to the new heaven and the new earth, where Christ will reign with his people in his place. Schreiner skillfully shows us the inseparability of God's kingdom, the cross of Jesus, and the gospel message. I highly recommend this interesting and encouraging book!"

Randy Alcorn, author, *Heaven*; *If God Is Good*; and *Hand in Hand*

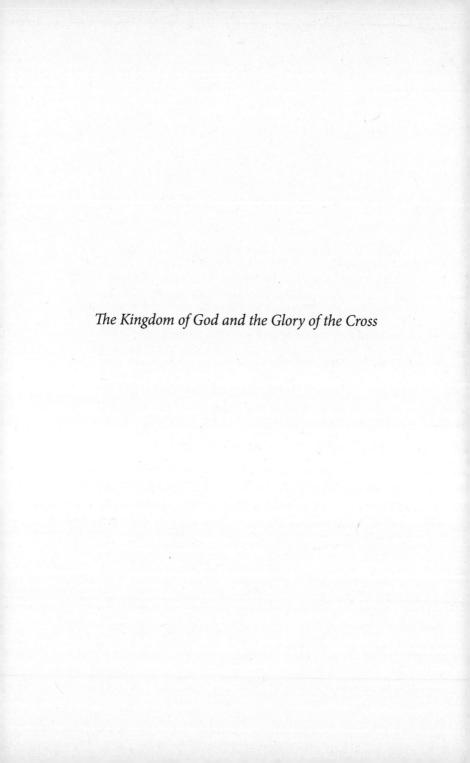

The Kingdom of God and the Glory of the Cross

The Kingdom of
God and the Glory
of the Cross

Patrick Schreiner

Dane C. Ortlund and Miles V. Van Pelt, series editors

WHEATON, ILLINOIS

The Kingdom of God and the Glory of the Cross

Copyright © 2018 by Patrick Schreiner

Published by Crossway
> 1300 Crescent Street
> Wheaton, Illinois 60187

Cover design: Jordan Singer

First printing 2018

Printed in the United States of America

Trade paperback ISBN: 978-1-4335-5823-8
ePub ISBN: 978-1-4335-5826-9
PDF ISBN: 978-1-4335-5824-5
Mobipocket ISBN: 978-1-4335-5825-2

Library of Congress Cataloging-in-Publication Data

Names: Schreiner, Patrick, author.
Title: The kingdom of God and the glory of the cross / Patrick Schreiner.
Description: Wheaton : Crossway, 2018. | Series: Short studies in biblical theology | Includes
    bibliographical references and index.
Identifiers: LCCN 2017025763 (print) | LCCN 2018002643 (ebook) | ISBN 9781433558245 (pdf) |
    ISBN 9781433558252 (mobi) | ISBN 9781433558269 (epub) | ISBN 9781433558238 (tp)
Subjects: LCSH: Kingdom of God--Biblical teaching.
Classification: LCC BS680.K52 (ebook) | LCC BS680.K52 S37 2018 (print) | DDC 231.7/2--dc23
LC record available at https://lccn.loc.gov/2017025763

BP		28	27	26	25	24	23	22	21	20	19	18
14	13	12	11	10	9	8	7	6	5	4	3	2

To my parents,
who modeled the kingdom life

Contents

Series Preface

Most of us tend to approach the Bible early on in our Christian lives as a vast, cavernous, and largely impenetrable book. We read the text piecemeal, finding golden nuggets of inspiration here and there, but remain unable to plug any given text meaningfully into the overarching storyline. Yet one of the great advances in evangelical biblical scholarship over the past few generations has been the recovery of biblical theology—that is, a renewed appreciation for the Bible as a theologically unified, historically rooted, progressively unfolding, and ultimately Christ-centered narrative of God's covenantal work in our world to redeem sinful humanity.

This renaissance of biblical theology is a blessing, yet little of it has been made available to the general Christian population. The purpose of Short Studies in Biblical Theology is to connect the resurgence of biblical theology at the academic level with everyday believers. Each volume is written by a capable scholar or churchman who is consciously writing in a way that requires no prerequisite theological training of the reader. Instead, any thoughtful Christian disciple can track with and benefit from these books.

Each volume in this series takes a whole-Bible theme and traces it through Scripture. In this way readers not only learn about a given theme but also are given a model for how to read the Bible as a coherent whole.

We are launching this series because we love the Bible, we love the church, and we long for the renewal of biblical theology in the academy to enliven the hearts and minds of Christ's disciples all around the world. As editors, we have found few discoveries more thrilling in life than that of seeing the whole Bible as a unified story of God's gracious acts of redemption, and indeed of seeing the whole Bible as ultimately about Jesus, as he himself testified (Luke 24:27; John 5:39).

The ultimate goal of Short Studies in Biblical Theology is to magnify the Savior and to build up his church—magnifying the Savior through showing how the whole Bible points to him and his gracious rescue of helpless sinners; and building up the church by strengthening believers in their grasp of these life-giving truths.

Dane C. Ortlund and Miles V. Van Pelt

Introduction

The Importance of the Kingdom

"What is the kingdom of God?"

The student leaned back and looked at me. I paused, fumbled around, then tossed out some words, but I ended my little incoherent bluster by saying that we would find out as we continued to study Matthew. This was back in college. My ministry director had asked me to lead a Bible study for students over the summer. I decided we would study Matthew. I had never studied Matthew before, and a tinge of trepidation ran down my spine, because the Epistles were my comfort zone. I knew the learning curve was going to be steep.

Although my life up to this moment had been filled with good Bible teaching, I felt misplaced in a foreign land when I came to the language of *kingdom*. I knew the basics of the gospel message, but I could not figure out how the kingdom of God related to it or why Jesus spoke so often of it. My view of the good news had been abstracted, and I had overlooked the narrative that stood beside and underneath the glorious doctrines of Christianity.

As I began to study the kingdom, I grasped that it was the thread that stitched the entire canon together. How could I have missed it? Why wasn't the concept clear to me before? The Bible is most fundamentally a narrative, and the kingdom of God is the thematic framework for that narrative.

Similarly, when many modern-day Christians come to kingdom language in the Bible, they have a hard time knowing what it is. Jesus never directly explains it; he never gives a definition, and the Gospel writers never record the crowds or disciples asking what it is. There seems to be an implicit assumption that everyone knows what the kingdom is.

Furthermore, kingdom language is pervasive in the Gospels, and the concept is strewn through the rest of the Bible. Jesus begins his ministry by announcing that the kingdom of God is at hand (Mark 1:15), and the Gospel writers encapsulate Jesus's ministry in the phrase "the gospel of the kingdom" (Matt. 4:23). Jesus's relentless focus on the kingdom provoked Gordon Fee to say:

> You cannot know anything about Jesus, anything, if you miss the kingdom of God. . . . You are zero on Jesus if you don't understand this term. I'm sorry to say it that strongly, but this is the great failure of evangelical Christianity. We have had Jesus without the kingdom of God, and therefore have literally done Jesus in.[1]

So rather than being a "zero on Jesus," many have attempted to get their arms around this idea of the kingdom. Unfortunately, the term has become the buzzword for everyone's pet issue. Since the kingdom is nowhere defined, people pour in their own meaning.

Some have equated it with heaven and said that Jesus was saying, in so many words, "The kingdom is the place you go when you

---

1. Gordon Fee, "Jesus: Early Ministry/Kingdom of God," lecture (1993), Regent College, tape series 2235E, pt. 1, Regent College, Vancouver, BC, Canada.

die." Others have understood kingdom as referring to the church. From their perspective, Jesus announced the beginning of the age of the church.[2] In this conception, the kingdom and the church are synonymous. Still others have seen the kingdom of God as simply ethics. Jesus's announcement is a call to social action. *The kingdom* thus becomes a term that denotes good deeds. Humankind builds the kingdom of God as it "works for the ideal social order and endeavors to solve the problems of poverty, sickness, labor relations, social inequalities, and race relations."[3]

Evangelicals, in particular, have been prone to reduce the kingdom to God's rule, power, or sovereignty.[4] George Eldon Ladd disseminated this view in his numerous works on the kingdom, arguing that the dynamic rule is the primary meaning.[5] In more popular evangelical circles the kingdom becomes a euphemism for the rule of God in one's heart. The kingdom thus coils into an inward, subjective mechanism, a secret power that enters the human soul and lays hold of it.

Regrettably, the defining characteristic of the kingdom in evangelicalism has been abstracted, and the time has come to restore the kingdom to its concrete nature. All the definitions above suffer from reductionism. They take a part of the whole and place it in the center. So how can we define the kingdom?

---

2. Mark D. Roberts, "What Was the Message of Jesus?," accessed December 28, 2017, http://patheos.com/blogs/markdroberts/series/what-was-the-message-of-jesus/.

3. George Eldon Ladd, *The Gospel of the Kingdom: Scriptural Studies in the Kingdom of God* (Grand Rapids, MI: Eerdmans, 1959), 16.

4. If they don't reduce the kingdom to God's rule, then they still argue that the kingdom is foremost about God's reign. See, e.g., Jeremy Treat, who argues, "The kingdom is foremost about God's reign; then human vice-regency; and then the realm of God's reign." Jeremy R. Treat, *The Crucified King: Atonement and Kingdom in Biblical and Systematic Theology* (Grand Rapids, MI: Zondervan, 2014), 40. Ridderbos implies that it might go back to the Reformers, saying, "Their viewpoint was theocentric, but in a rather static manner. The historical and eschatological aspects of the biblical revelation of the Kingdom of God were not prominent in their theology." Herman N. Ridderbos, *When the Time Had Fully Come: Studies in New Testament Theology* (Grand Rapids, MI: Eerdmans, 1957), 10.

5. He did assert that the kingdom derivatively refers to a realm. G. E. Ladd, "Kingdom of God—Reign or Realm,?" *Journal of Biblical Literature* 81 (September 1, 1962): 236.

The Kingdom Tree

Since we never get a textbook definition of the kingdom in the Bible, some help in understanding the kingdom can be found in examining one of the images that the Scriptures regularly associate with the kingdom: a tree. The Bible begins and ends with the figure of a tree. Genesis speaks of the tree of life that springs from the ground at the voice of the Lord and the forbidden tree of good and evil (Gen. 2:9). Watering these trees are the rivers that flow out of the garden. At the end of Scripture, the tree of life rises again, positioned within the holy city that has twelve gates, high walls, and a river running through it. Revelation describes the tree as having leaves that heal the nations (Rev. 22:2).

But the tree imagery does not merely bracket the Scriptures; it tracks its way through the entire Bible. In the Old Testament, King Nebuchadnezzar dreams about a tree that grows strong, and its top reaches the heavens so that all nations can see it (Dan. 4:10–12). Daniel interprets the dream for Nebuchadnezzar, explaining to him that the tree is a symbol of his kingdom, which will be taken away from him.

The great prophet Isaiah also speaks of a tree, yet this tree has been reduced to a stump. From this stump of Jesse comes forth a branch (Isa. 11:1). King David pronounces that those who rely on the word of God are like a tree that grows and flourishes (Ps. 1:3). In the Gospels Jesus regularly compares the kingdom to a tree (Matt. 13:31; Mark 4:31–32).

One particular tree alters the skyline of the Gospels. Just as the tree was the undoing of Adam and Eve in the garden, so the cross ends Jesus's life. He hangs upon this tree for the world to mock and sneer. This tree secures the nails that pierce his hands and feet. Rome, the Jewish leaders, and Satan assume that Jesus's kingdom has been conquered by nailing Jesus to the cross, yet in a scandalous twist, this tree becomes the King's greatest victory.

There drapes the sign that declares, "This is Jesus, the King of the Jews" (Matt. 27:37). The defeat of Adam and Eve is the victory of God; the Serpent's sting is Christ's great victory. The tree shaped like a cross is the fulcrum of God summing up all things in heaven and on earth. It is positioned vertically, and Jesus's hands stretch out horizontally, harmonizing north, south, east, and west through Jesus's disfigured body.[6] The tree is, as Revelation portrays it, healing for the nations.

The tree in the Scriptures thus becomes representative of the concept of which Jesus speaks so often: the kingdom. If the tree is a symbol for the kingdom throughout the Scriptures, then what does it teach us about the nature of the kingdom?

First, the image of the tree in Scripture communicates power, rule, or sovereignty. Large trees symbolize power and strength. The tree in the garden promises life. If Adam and Eve were to eat from it, they would be like God. Nebuchadnezzar's tree, in a similar way, reaches up to the heavens and is visible to the whole world. In Revelation, there is a city with high walls, and the tree stands in the middle of this city as a symbol of power and strength.

Second, the tree usually has some relationship or connection with people. The tree of Nebuchadnezzar has creatures resting beneath its branches, with Nebuchadnezzar as the head representative of the people. In Isaiah, the branch shooting forth from the stump is quickly identified with a person (Isa. 11:2). The leaves of the tree in Revelation heal the nations. The tree in Psalm 1 is also a metaphor for a person.

Third, the image of the tree always implies the idea of *place*.[7] The tree is placed in the garden. The tree in Daniel is placed where the whole world can see the top of it. In Revelation the tree is in

---

6. Historical records show that the arms of those crucified were probably not stretched out precisely horizontally, but they were still in the general horizontal direction.

7. Stephen Dempster articulated the concept of people and place with the terms *dominion* and *dynasty* as well as *geography* and *genealogy*, *land* and *lineage*. Stephen Dempster, *Dominion and Dynasty: A Theology of the Hebrew Bible*, New Studies in Biblical Theology (Downers Grove, IL: IVP Academic, 2003).

the center of the city. Now, this tree imagery throughout Scripture may just be that—tree imagery. But this symbol can and should be instructive for us.

Defining the Kingdom

So, expanding beyond the abstract notion of the kingdom as mere sovereignty, I will use the following definition of the kingdom in this study: *The kingdom is the King's power over the King's people in the King's place.*[8] These three realities (power, people, place) interrelate, and although they can be distinguished, they never can be separated.[9] They are like strands of a rope tightly twisted together.

Some might object, "Shouldn't power be primary, because without rule or authority people and place cannot come into being?" But the same can be said for all three. Kings rule over places and people. Power is empty without people and place. Place also affects people, and people affect place. Power is in places, and places themselves wield power. This interrelationship between the three is not meant to bewilder but to show that these concepts are closely related; we can't rip one of them out and use it as a *primary* definition or description of the kingdom.[10]

Usually, studies on the kingdom concentrate on two interrelated subjects. They emphasize the kingdom as God's rule and stress the temporal question, Is the kingdom now or in the future? Little atten-

---

8. The first time I read something similar to this was Graeme Goldsworthy, *The Goldsworthy Trilogy: Gospel and Kingdom, Gospel and Wisdom, The Gospel in Revelation* (Exeter, UK: Paternoster, 2011), 53–54. He defines the kingdom as "God's people, in God's place, under God's rule." Waltke similarly says, "A nation consists of a common people, sharing a common land, submissive to a common law, and having a common ruler." Bruce Waltke, "The Kingdom of God in Biblical Theology," in *Looking to the Future: Evangelical Essays in Eschatology*, ed. David W. Baker (Grand Rapids, MI: Baker, 2011), 18.

9. For the sake of simplicity, I am keeping my definition trifold. Yet if I were to add any two pieces, they would be the king's *presence* and the king's *law* (or precepts).

10. I have heard some argue that the people and the place of the kingdom are not to be equated with the kingdom although they are inseparable from it. But could we not propose the same question for the power? Should the kingdom be equated with power, or is it merely inseparable from it? I find that trying to divide these concepts in a hierarchy ultimately fails logical tests.

tion is given to the *where* or *space* or *people* of the kingdom. For too long, scholars have chided that Jesus's kingdom does not concern geography or locale. So while we need to include the ideas of power, rule, and strength, in the Scriptures these are not merely abstract concepts; they are life-giving realities.

The tree in Psalm 1 grows and is nourished by the stream of the Word of God. The tree of life's leaves give the nations healing and life in Revelation. The tree in Daniel allows the animals to lie beneath its shade. Power is not about coercion; it is about structures for flourishing. God created the tree of life out of his power so that Adam and Eve could flourish as human beings, but they turned to the forbidden tree. Power and sovereignty in the Scriptures are linked to creation, protection, and the flourishing of people.

In addition, the kingdom must include people—namely, a king and his subjects. The king is representative of the people, and the king also provides shelter and safety for the people through his kingdom. God's kingdom will *contain* and be realized *through* God's image bearers as servant kings. As Gerhard Lohfink said, "A king without a people is no king at all but a figure in a museum."[11] Therefore, it would be wise not to downplay the people aspect of a kingdom.

In the same way, a kingdom must be a realm. A king without a territory is an enigma. The place of the kingdom cannot be erased from the description and definition, just as a city must be situated. I. Howard Marshall said concerning the kingdom, "While it has been emphasized almost *ad nauseam* that the primary concept is that of the sovereignty of kingship or actual rule of God and not of a territory ruled by a king, it must also be emphasized that kingship cannot be exercised in the abstract."[12]

---

11. Gerhard Lohfink, *Jesus of Nazareth: What He Wanted, Who He Was*, trans. Linda Maloney (Collegeville, MN: Liturgical, 2012), 25.

12. I. Howard Marshall, "Church," in *Dictionary of Jesus and the Gospels*, ed. J. B. Green and S. McKnight (Downers Grove, IL: InterVarsity, 1992), 123.

So what is the kingdom? It is concrete; it is earthy; it is people; it is place; it is about Jesus; it concerns the cross; it is about the new heavens and the new earth; it is about community, politics, order, bodies, and human flourishing. It is about power, family, thrones, walls, gates, rivers, and streams. The kingdom is cosmic in scope, and to close the door on the vast picture that the Scriptures use to paint the kingdom is to misinterpret and misunderstand the goal of redemption. In the kingdom of Christ, the ransomed will be in the presence of God living under the law of the King. The kingdom is the basic edifice for entering the story of the Scriptures. The aim of this study is to investigate the rich concept of kingdom across the storyline of Scripture.

Consequences of a Partial Definition

Why is it imperative to define the kingdom as "power, people, and place"? Is this just a precision issue that scholars can argue about? At least three consequences arise if we neglect people and place and focus only on power.

First, without people and place, the kingdom becomes intangible. Christians sometimes disparage the material world. Although alterations to this view are making progress, at times physicality is still belittled. Yet the kingdom is never presented as an immaterial entity in the Scriptures. Recognizing the importance of people and place brings a groundedness to kingdom language. The incarnation and resurrection of Jesus are the key theological doctrines that affirm this rootedness. As N. D. Wilson said, "If [God] wanted a spiritual kingdom, He could have saved Himself a huge amount of trouble by just skipping Christmas."[13]

The second consequence that befalls us if we neglect place and

---

13. N. D. Wilson, *Death by Living: Life Is Meant to Be Spent* (Nashville, TN: Thomas Nelson, 2103), 77.

people is that we might truncate our understanding of the mission of the church. If the kingdom is merely God's sovereignty, then what role do his people play? Do they exist only to tell others about the King's power? The mission of the church is to bring people in union with a real King and into a real kingdom, not just to assent to some immaterial theocracy. Disciples are people who go out and give shape to every space. Jesus brings people into place, and he gives them a law that structures their interactions. If the mission of the church is reduced to an intellectual assent of a sovereign God but does not mold how we use our hands and feet, then the church and the kingdom become a monastery rather than a world-forming force. The kingdom of God is the mission of God, and we must not limit this mission.

Third, and related, if we define kingdom as mere power, we slash through most of the pages of the kingdom story and misrepresent it. If *kingdom* is a term used to summarize what is happening in the narrative of Scripture, then it would be unwise to reduce this narrative to the notion of sovereignty. The Scriptures are all about the people of Israel and the places in which they reside. The entire Old Testament can be summarized in this way. This story comes to a climax through the King who cleanses Israel's land and puts the law within their hearts so that they can flourish on this earth under the rule of the King.

The end of the book of Revelation points to a kingdom with a King and his subjects who live in the garden city of the new heavens and the new earth. Revelation does not end with souls soaring in the sky but with a canvas of city construction. There are dozens of helpful books on the kingdom, but many stumble through or entirely ignore the Wisdom Literature, Paul's letters, and other portions of Scripture. To remove these sections of Scripture from a biblical theology tears out the heart of the Bible. A holistic definition allows us to stitch the Bible back together.

The Aim and Method

If the kingdom is the *thematic framework* for all the Scriptures with all other themes orbiting around it, then how does one approach a biblical theology of the kingdom? A short study such as this on a biblical theology of the kingdom must pick and choose which peaks in the Scriptures are worth ascending, surveying the summits and climbing a few, while painfully passing by others. To navigate the terrain, we will do the following.

1. Limit discussion to key events, prophecies, and seams of Scripture that carry the kingdom story forward but also attempt to survey the variety of presentations in the Bible.

2. Explain various aspects of the definition of the kingdom, working to do justice to the biblical descriptions, images, and symbols of the kingdom.

3. Attempt to give equal attention to each major section of Scripture. This means that the Wisdom Literature, Acts, and the Pauline Epistles receive more attention than you might expect. This is intentional. Most biblical theologies that speak of the kingdom have embarrassingly little to say about these sections.

4. Follow the ordering of the Hebrew Scriptures, which divide the Old Testament into three sections: the Law, the Prophets, and the Writings. Most of our English Bibles follow what is called the "Christian" ordering of the Old Testament. Yet most early Jews read what we would call the "Hebrew" ordering of the Old Testament. When in Luke 24:44 Jesus mentions "the Law of Moses and the Prophets and the Psalms," he is referencing the

Hebrew ordering of the Law, the Prophets, and the Writings. Although this is not the only way to order the Old Testament canon (the Christian ordering also has historical attestation), the Hebrew order does highlight some unique kingdom themes. The differences of order can be seen in the chart below.

English Bible Order	Hebrew Bible Order
Pentateuch	**Law**
Genesis Exodus Leviticus Numbers Deuteronomy	Genesis Exodus Leviticus Numbers Deuteronomy
Historical Books	**Prophets**
Joshua Judges Ruth 1–2 Samuel 1–2 Kings Ezra Nehemiah Esther	Joshua Judges Samuel Kings Isaiah Jeremiah Ezekiel Book of the Twelve (Minor Prophets)
Poetry	**Writings**
Job Psalms Proverbs Ecclesiastes Song of Solomon	Psalms Job Proverbs Ruth Song of Solomon Ecclesiastes Lamentations Esther Daniel Ezra Nehemiah Chronicles
Prophets	
Isaiah Jeremiah Lamentations Ezekiel Daniel Twelve Minor Prophets	

In this volume, we will consider our theme based on the following chart:

Law	Reviving hope in the kingdom
Prophets	Foreshadowing the kingdom
Writings	Life in the kingdom
Gospels	Embodying the kingdom
Acts and Epistles	Kingdom community
Revelation	Achieving the kingdom goal

More specifically, we will focus on how people and place must be included with power in a definition of *kingdom*. I am arguing in essence that this definition goes all the way from the beginning to the end. It crosses through the books of Moses, the Prophets, and the Wisdom Literature and finds its climax in Jesus's life, death, resurrection, ascension, and exaltation. Although the term *kingdom* is used sparingly in the Epistles, the concept constitutes the framework for Paul's worldview. Once you see it, it is hard to unsee.

The Threshold of the Scriptures

What better place to begin a study on the kingdom than with the King himself? Matthew begins the New Testament with eight Greek words that instruct readers on how to put their Bibles together. It teaches us how to read both backward and forward: "The book of the genealogy of Jesus Christ, the son of David, the son of Abraham" (Matt. 1:1).

Because of its placement at the beginning of the New Testament, Matthew 1 can be understood as the threshold through which one enters the doorway of Scripture. This opening genealogy highlights the important themes of king, kingdom, and people. Although the term *kingdom* does not occur in Matthew's genealogy, the concept of king is hard to miss. Matthew shapes our conception of Jesus by presenting him as the son of David—the successor to the kingly throne.

Two clues in the genealogy confirm this. First, in 1:6 Matthew identifies David as "the king." The noun here appears with a definite article—meaning David was not merely a king, but *the* king. Second, the entire structure of the genealogy is planned through David, who was promised an everlasting kingdom. Matthew's lineage is the royal book of origin; David is the king of Israel to whom an everlasting kingdom was promised.

Jesus comes as the king in David's line who will bring the people back from exile and unite the kingdom again. The New Testament begins with the announcement that Jesus is *the* King. Matthew instructs his readers that kingship and kingdom are the major themes through which to view both Old and New Testaments. All the other themes of Scripture find their ultimate meaning in this reality.

Second, the opening words "the book of the genealogy" occur elsewhere in a similar fashion only in the book of Genesis (Gen. 2:4; 5:1). Genesis 2:4 is about the origin of heaven and earth (place), while 5:1 is about the origin of Adam and Eve (people). Matthew thus indicates at the start of his Gospel that the new creation (with people and place as his guiding concepts) is accomplished by King Jesus. The King is the one who will restore Israel to their home. As readers encounter the genealogy, the restoration of the kingdom comes into focus as Matthew traces out their history through the Babylonian exile. The Babylonian exile shapes the assembly of the genealogy. So, in the first words of the New Testament, Matthew highlights the King and the kingdom as the guiding concepts for reading the Scriptures.

The messianic King is the epicenter of this new creation and new humanity. The rest of Matthew's story explains the King's mission. He is granted authority, he rescues Israel, and he creates a new home. The cursed tree becomes the means to the kingdom, and all authority in heaven and on earth is given to him so that his followers can go out into all places (all nations) and spread the gospel of the kingdom in the name of the Father, the Son, and the Holy Spirit.

So, although the word *kingdom* is not used in the introduction of Matthew's Gospel, the idea is present right below the surface. The story of the Bible is the story of the King and his kingdom. As Dan McCartney says, the arrival of the kingdom of God is the "reinstatement of the originally intended divine order for the earth, with man properly situated as God's vice-regent."[14] Jesus is the true human receiving, embodying, bringing, inaugurating, and fulfilling the kingdom promises.

---

14. Dan McCartney, "Ecce Homo: The Coming of the Kingdom as the Restoration of Human Vicegerency," *Westminster Theological Journal* 56.1 (1994): 2.

PART 1

KINGDOM IN THE OLD TESTAMENT

1

The Law

Reviving Hope in the Kingdom

The closing lines of Norman Maclean's celebrated novel *A River Runs Through It* are known for their beauty but also their mystical and enigmatic meaning:

> Eventually, all things merge into one, and a river runs through it. The river was cut by the world's great flood and runs over rocks from the basement of time. On some of those rocks are timeless raindrops. Under the rocks are the words, and some of the words are theirs. I am haunted by waters.[1]

Water and Words

The two key symbols in Maclean's work merge in this passage: water and words. The river is the backdrop to his narrative, but Maclean

---

1. Norman Maclean, *A River Runs Through It* (Chicago: University of Chicago Press, 1989), 161.

understands that under the watery rocks are words. Words shape the reality of the river of his life.

In a similar way, the Hebrew Scriptures start with water and words. God as the King, through his words, separates the water from the dry land, setting up a place to put his people to form his kingdom. The water feeds the tree of the kingdom in Genesis, eventually spilling over into Revelation. All things merge as the river flows out from the throne of God and the Lamb and nourishes the trees of the land (Rev. 22:1). But underneath this water lie words, words from the Creator to shape the ebb and flow of the growth and decline of the kingdom.

My aim in this chapter is to show you that Jesus did not invent the concept of kingdom. Rather, it started in the garden and has always concerned people, place, and power. The earth was divinely designed to serve as the place of the kingdom for the people of the kingdom. Beginning the first act of this narrative is the Law (Pentateuch), which voices how kingdom hope thrives, is corrupted, and then revives; stories of failure, hope, swindling, faithfulness, murder, and trust gather momentum as the tapestry of God's drama for all of creation unfolds.

The Kingdom Story in the Law	
Creation	Establishing the kingdom
Fall	Corrupting the kingdom
Call of Abraham	Reviving hope in the kingdom

Kings and Queens

In the beginning God creates people and place by his power.[2] God separates the heavens and the earth, bringing order out of chaos. He

---

2. As Merrill writes, "The kingdom story begins with the first sentence in the Bible: 'In the beginning God created the heavens and the earth.' By this simple but majestic affirmation, both king and realm are introduced; and in the six days that follow, the citizens of the kingdom, inanimate and animate, appear in their course until mankind, the crowning glory of the Creator, takes center stage. . . . The stage has been set, the players are ready, and the drama may now begin." Eugene H. Merrill, *Everlasting Dominion: A Theology of the Old Testament* (Nashville, TN: B&H Academic, 2006), 278.

populates the earth with animals, but the crown of his creation is humankind. Man and woman are formed from the dust of the earth, establishing an enduring connection between the ground and mankind. Adam and Eve are given tasks to be fruitful and multiply, to fill the earth and subdue it, and to have dominion over it. Humankind enjoys the presence of God and is to extend the blessings of God's fellowship to all of creation.

Adam and Eve are made to be king and queen. While God is the definitive King, because he is the Creator and his kingly rule is universal, he makes Adam and Eve to be those who carry out his rule. They are also to rule the earth and bring order as God has done. God includes them in his world-forming, kingdom-creating plan. Although the early narratives of Adam and Eve do not explicitly label them as king and queen, at least two hints in the text give that effect.

First, Adam and Eve are created in the image and likeness of God. The idea of image and likeness communicates two main ideas: (1) kingship and (2) sonship. In the ancient world, kings were depicted as representing or constituting the image of God, so they ruled on behalf of God. These ancient kings were characterized as images of the gods, and as living images they maintained or destroyed cosmic harmony. The kingdom concept began with Adam and Eve in the garden; they were God's subjects made to rule the world.

The second hint that they are to be kings and queens is that God placed Adam and Eve in the garden, the temple of God's presence, and tells them to "work" and "keep" the garden (Gen. 2:15). These same Hebrew terms, rendered here in Genesis as "work" and "keep," are combined elsewhere in the Old Testament to explain the priests' role in the temple (see Num. 3:7–8; 8:26; 18:5–6). Adam and Eve are to maintain the created order of the sacred space of the sanctuary, filling and subduing the world (Gen. 1:28). Garden and temple expansion is the King's plan to conquer the outer chaotic sphere with order and goodness. Adam and Eve are to administrate the kingdom under God's authority, forming the earth and bringing flourishing to all nations.

In a tragic twist, Adam and Eve seek to usurp God's authority. They reject God's kingdom and eat from the tree of the knowledge of good and evil. There were two trees in the garden: the tree of life and this tree of death. Adam and Eve chose the tree of death and were cast from the place where God's presence dwelt.

The kingdom plan was *corrupted* when a rival kingdom slithered into the ear of Eve and Adam. The vice-regents, who were to carry out God's blueprint for all of creation, chose to follow the Serpent and personally offend the King of the universe. Now chaos and sin frustrate the desire to rule the earth and subdue it. False kingdoms are instantly part of the picture. Every generation afterward will face the same choice: which kind of kingdom will they construct?

God's judgment on Adam and Eve is displacement from the garden; his redemption will have to include re-placement. This re-placement can come only through a new king. Adam and Eve have failed as king and queen, and a new king is needed to set things right in creation.

God promises Eve that one of her children will be this new king (Gen. 3:15). Only through this enigmatic "seed" will God bring restoration to all of creation, but the offspring of Adam and Eve will continually war against the Serpent until the promised child crushes the head of the Serpent. As Dempster says, "This battle will determine who will have dominion over the created order."[3]

The rest of the book of Genesis—indeed, the whole canon—is set up to fulfill this promise of a coming King. Genesis is structured around genealogies of the progress of the seed. Humanity is to bring place into being by living according to the rules of their king. They

---

3. Stephen Dempster, *Dominion and Dynasty: A Theology of the Hebrew Bible*, New Studies in Biblical Theology (Downers Grove, IL: IVP Academic, 2003), 69.

are, in some sense, to construct the kingdom. Unfortunately, the Old Testament shows that all of Adam's offspring fail in this task.

The Downward Spiral of Genesis 3–11

Adam's commission to be the king to rule the earth and expand the temple is passed onto his offspring. But so is his rebellious nature. God gives the kingly commission to Noah and his sons (Gen. 9:1, 7), to Abraham (Gen. 12:2; 17:2, 6, 8, 16), to Isaac (Gen. 26:3–4, 24), to Jacob (Gen. 28:3–4, 14), and to the nation of Israel (Deut. 7:13), indicating that each successive generation is conceived of as royalty. The genealogies in Genesis chart both the progress and regress of the seed and show God's faithfulness to his promises despite the mutiny of his children. Some of Adam's seed are chosen to bring blessings; others are not: it is Seth, not Cain; Shem, not Canaan; Abraham, not Nahor; Isaac, not Ishmael; Jacob, not Esau.[4]

Because God endowed humanity with royal authority, that authority could also be warped. While the people of God seek to bring the kingdom to earth, their striving only compounds their plight. Genesis 3–11 pictures the downward spiral of Adam's children. They become autonomous kings with selfish rather than selfless desires, and the people-to-people strife affects the locale of the kingdom, as it always does.

Cain murders his brother Abel in Genesis 4. God curses Cain from the very ground that received his brother's blood. Cain is made to wander and flee his home, the opposite of a king dwelling in safety in his palace. Reliving his parents' fall, Cain's sin triggers an avalanche of chaos that fills the earth. Therefore, God decides that the time has come to clear the earth and start over with a righteous man.

God sends the flood in Genesis 6 as a sign of his judgment upon

---

4. Bruce Waltke, "The Kingdom of God in the Old Testament: Definitions and Story," in *The Kingdom of God*, Theology in Community (Wheaton, IL: Crossway, 2012), 62.

the kingdoms of the earth who have turned to their own ways. There is a righteous seed left—Noah and his family are saved on a boat and called to be fruitful and multiply and fill the earth, just as Adam was (Gen. 9:1, 7). Noah and his family are the new rulers on the earth.

The cycle of creation and de-creation continues. God creates; God's people destroy; he restores. Just as Adam and Eve's garden was on a mountain (Ezek. 28:14), so too Noah's new creation begins on Mount Ararat. Afterward the people attempt to establish a kingdom of their own. Noah eats of the vine instead of the tree. His children endeavor to build a tower with its top to the heavens so that they can make a name for themselves (Gen. 11:4). Unified but rebellious, humanity seeks to build a kingdom without God—in defiance of their King.

God's plan to dwell with humanity, and with humanity serving as stewards of his kingdom, has been warped. The fruit of Adam and Eve's rebellion is that people are in strife, and the places they seek to establish are frustrated by overgrown weeds. The ground works against them, and the bearing of children comes with pain. However, God's kingdom purpose will be not thwarted. God's plan will continue in those who believe he will work all things for their good and bring them into a good place.

Kingdom Hope Revived in Abraham

The miserable backdrop of the Tower of Babel is not the final gasp of the good kingdom. In Genesis 12 the kingdom hope is *revived* as God's covenant with Abraham sets into motion the fulfillment of the promise made in the garden about a King who will come and conquer the Serpent. The Serpent killer will come through the seed of Abraham. Through this covenant relationship God will establish his rule, resulting in blessings to people and places. So Abraham, like Adam, is cast as a kingly figure (Gen. 12:2–3; 17:2, 6, 8, 16; 22:18), and he will bear royal descendants ("Kings shall come from you," Gen. 17:6).

God promises to make Abraham into a great nation, to bless him, to make his name great so that he will be a blessing (Gen. 12:1). The parallels with Adam leap off the page.[5] Just as Adam was to extend the blessings of God to all people across the whole earth, so Abraham is going to be made into a great nation to bless all people. In Genesis 3–11 the word *curse* is used five times to portray the effects of sin. Now in Genesis 12:2–3 the word *bless* returns five times to make clear that God intends to reverse the curse. Abraham is to leave his land, but he will obtain more land; he is to leave his kindred, but God will make him into a great nation; he is to leave his Father's house, but he will become a blessing to all people. Abraham will be a blessing to all nations by being a kind, just, and fair ruler like God. God revives the kingdom hope through the covenant he makes with Abraham.

Concepts	Power	People	Place
Abraham leaves . . .	. . . his father's house	his kindred	his country
Abraham obtains . . .	. . . blessing to all people = ruler	great nation	land

The narrative continues to portray Abraham as a kingly figure. Abraham goes out and fights for Lot and conquers other kings. Even the king of Salem (Melchizedek) comes out to meet him and blesses him, calling him the possessor of heaven and earth (Gen. 14:19). But before Abraham can be made into a great kingdom, he must have his first child. The seed, the people of the king, must continue.

---

5. The same commission that is given to Adam, Noah, and Abraham is passed down to Isaac (Gen. 26:3–4, 24), Jacob (Gen. 28:3–4, 14; 35:11–12; 48:3, 15–16), and corporate Israel (Gen. 47:27; Deut. 7:13). Gordon Wenham says, "What Abram was promised was the hope of many an oriental monarch." Gordon John Wenham, John D. W. Watts, and Ralph P. Martin, *Genesis 1–15*, ed. David Allen Hubbard and Glenn W. Barker, Word Biblical Commentary (Grand Rapids, MI: Zondervan, 2014), 275.

Although God makes his promise to Abraham in Genesis 12, not until nine chapters (and twenty-five years!) later is Isaac born. Isaac is given the same promise that God had made to Abraham (Gen. 26:3–5). The text explicitly says that the whole earth will be blessed as a result of Abraham's obedience. God was searching for a righteous steward of his kingdom, and because Abraham believed God, it was counted to Abraham as righteousness (Gen. 15:6).

If one figure, beyond Adam and Eve, serves as a focal point upon which the rest of the kingdom story expands, it is Abraham. The rest of the Scriptures detail how the promise to Abraham springs to life through the wandering, disobedience, and victory of the people of Abraham. Joined with this emphasis is the journey of the seed toward the Promised Land, their occupation of the land, and their eventual exile from the land.

The reason Abraham is so important is that, like Adam, he is a kingly figure and the instrument through which God will establish his kingdom upon the earth. God's desire is to bring harmony to all things. What Adam disrupted, Abraham's family will mend.

Preservation of the Seed

The hope of the kingdom was revived with the promises made to Abraham. The rest of Genesis consequently concentrates on the preservation of Abraham's seed through various tragedies, mistakes, and sins. The greatness of Abraham's family is not in their wealth, strength, cunning, or even their faithfulness. No, Abraham's family becomes great because God is loyal to his promises—*he* safeguards the lives of Jacob and Joseph. Joseph's story, in particular, is about the conservation of the sons of Abraham despite the evil actions of Joseph's brothers selling him into slavery (Gen. 50:22). Joseph finds himself in Egypt and eventually rises to second-in-command.

However, God's immediate purpose is for Joseph to provide food for the sons of Abraham when a seven-year famine hits the whole earth. As a result of the famine, the people of Abraham move to Egypt to be sustained. Before Genesis ends, we see Jacob gather his children and bless them. He singles out his son Judah and promises him kingship in the last days. "The scepter shall not depart from Judah, / nor the ruler's staff from between his feet, / until tribute comes to him; / and to him shall be the obedience of the peoples" (Gen. 49:10). A new king is coming, and he will come from the loins of Judah.

Exodus begins by noting how great and numerous the people of Abraham had become in Egypt, and because of that, the Egyptians begin to fear the people of Israel and thus mistreat them. The sword of the Serpent and the sword of the seed clash against one another. The kings, from each respective line, will war with one another until the last great battle. In the grand narrative, Egypt was a pit stop for Israel; the promise to Abraham was that his descendants would have their land, and to have their land, they needed to get out of Egypt.

So God releases them from slavery in Egypt by his great redemption and takes them on a journey to their land. Although the land was an end, it was not the end in itself. The land was to be a place of rest and security, ensuring that the people could worship their God and also be a blessing to other nations. The story of the garden kingdom had not been dropped from the narrative. On the contrary, it had just begun.

The Law of the King

When God rescues the people out of Egypt, he first leads them to Mount Sinai to give them the law (*torah*). Readers regularly begin to lose the kingdom story here. What is the point of this law in relationship to the kingdom?

Ancient Near Eastern kings regularly gave their people legal treatises or laws to sanctify the people and encourage justice with their neighbors. In the same way, God gave covenantal instruction to his people so that they would serve as subrulers of his kingdom on earth, as they ought. God's objective was always to establish his kingdom on the earth, and the law was meant to form not only personal ethics but also a community.

The Mosaic covenant demonstrates God's determination to advance his kingdom on the earth through his people. The law given at Sinai directs, guides, and instructs the people in their spread of justice and peace (*shalom*) and worship of him. Thus, Moses commands parents to teach their children the Torah, because their retention of the land is dependent upon it (Deut. 6:1–9).

The people are designated as a "kingdom of priests" and a "holy nation" (Ex. 19:6). Readers should immediately think of God's instruction to Adam and Eve as kings and priests. This description is both a reality and a goal that the people are to strive for. With the language of kingdom here, it is clear: the law coheres with what God will do on the grand scale. By obeying the law God's people will become a true "kingdom of priests," thereby serving God and all of creation. "Israel will thus redefine the meaning of dominion—service."[6]

They will also be a holy nation. The term *nation* is parallel to the term *kingdom* and thus an economic and political term. A *holy* nation is one set apart and consecrated for God. His people are consecrated to act as his stewards in the kingdom by following the law. The law does not suspend or halt the kingdom narrative; it advances the kingdom promises to both Adam and Abraham.

Law and kingdom are twin siblings; the law pushes readers to connect what was happening at Sinai with the rest of the narrative. God was constructing a community, a nation, through which he would reign, and his people would govern with him, bringing order

---

6. Dempster, *Dominion and Dynasty*, 101–2.

to a disordered world. If the people followed the law, then the kingdom of heaven would disrupt the kingdoms of this earth and reestablish Eden. The Torah was the King's instruction manual to his vice-regents. If the kingdom was a tree, then the Torah watered its roots. But how specifically was this weak, failing nation to disrupt the kingdoms of this earth?

Leviticus answers that question, giving in-depth instructions about what it means to be a holy people of a holy God. The book divides into two sections: (1) laws of the tabernacle (Lev. 1:1–16:34), and (2) laws of the community (Lev. 17:1–27:34)—in other words, laws concerning *place* and laws concerning *people*. The people are to keep the place of tabernacle in such a way as to mirror God's dwelling, and they are to act amongst themselves so as to reflect a holy King. Communing with God is to be the means to bless all nations.

Although Leviticus divides into two parts, the two parts are related. If the tabernacle is not prepared, the nation will not be fit to meet God. If the nation is not suitable, then the tabernacle will be defiled. As L. Michael Morales notes, "Life with God in the house of God—this was the original goal of the creation of the cosmos, and which then became the goal of redemption."[7] If this was the goal, Leviticus specifies the means of that goal: prepare the house, prepare the nation. Dwelling with God also means ruling with God. The book of Leviticus expresses how the people can be holy and thus rule with their holy God. The specifics of the Torah, given from their true King, are explained in marvelous detail because God would construct his kingdom through his people.

But the narrative about the Torah is not all positive. Again and again it is clear that the people *could not* keep the law, so a partial solution is provided. At the very center of Leviticus is the Day of

---

7. L. Michael Morales, *Who Shall Ascend the Mountain of the Lord? A Biblical Theology of the Book of Leviticus* (Nottingham, UK: IVP Academic, 2015), 17.

Atonement. If the aim of Leviticus is to point the people toward dwelling with God, then the means by which that will happen is the Day of Atonement. The life of the flesh is in the blood, and it is by the blood, by the life of another life, that one makes atonement (Lev. 17:11). Through the life of another the divine presence of God is enjoyed. Once atonement has been made, God's people can enter into the Most Holy Place, which represents fullness of life.[8]

The kingdom includes people, but they must be *remade people*, different from their forefathers who rejected God's kingship. God remakes his people through the Torah and sacrifice. Unfortunately the law also points to how they fail to be kings and queens. To enter the presence of God, to be the people of God, to be in the place of God, to be the kingdom of priests and the holy nation, blood must be poured out, for they cannot keep his precepts.

Sacrifice is the center of the kingdom plan.

Seeking Their Home

Leviticus depicts the details of God's kingdom plan, but Numbers continues where the narrative of Exodus leaves off. Numbers is framed with the theme of "generations," which recalls Genesis and the progress of the seed. It begins with a generation that should have entered the Land of Promise but has failed to do so because of unbelief. Numbers closes with a census of a new generation poised to inherit the land. Thus, the book of Numbers is about the people of Israel and their journey to occupy their kingdom.

However, that is not all the book is about. "The strength of Israel did not ultimately come from its army. Israel's uniqueness and power came from the presence of the Lord in their midst."[9] The power and

---

8. Ibid., 31.
9. Thomas R. Schreiner, *The King in His Beauty: A Biblical Theology of the Old and New Testaments* (Grand Rapids, MI: Baker Academic, 2013), 68. Can I quote my dad? Yes, I can. I just did.

presence of their King is central to the story, but it is a power operating for the nation if they obey the covenant.

Unfortunately, as in Genesis and Exodus, Numbers develops the theme of the disobedience of the seed of Adam. They complain about their circumstances (Num. 11:1–3), they grumble about eating manna all day (Num. 11:4–10), they are paralyzed by fear (Num. 13:28–29, 31–34), and they turn against their leaders. In sum, they fail to believe the Lord despite all he has done for them.

So the Lord threatens to destroy the people and raise up a new generation, but Moses intercedes for the people. Sparing the people from utter destruction, God's judgment on them is obstruction from the Promised Land (Num. 14:21–23). Longing for their land is a theme woven throughout the Pentateuch. Adam was displaced from the garden, Jacob's family was displaced in Egypt, and here Israel is made to live in the wilderness.

However, the disobedience of the people does not nullify the kingdom promises God had made to his people. While the wilderness generation is judged, a new generation is coming that will occupy the land (Numbers 21–36). Moses intercedes for them by lifting up a bronze serpent, and all who look upon the serpent are healed. The odd symbol implies that the way to the land is through death. Only through looking death in the face will people be able to enter the kingdom. Life comes by passing through death.

Numbers begins with the people sitting on the edge of the land. Yet only those who obey, albeit imperfectly, will inherit what the Lord has promised. The land is reminiscent of Eden, with palm groves that stretch afar, like gardens beside a river, like cedar trees beside the waters (Num. 24:6).

The disobedience of the people does not ultimately cancel out the promises God had made to both Adam and Abraham, although there are immediate consequences. Even the pagan prophet Balaam speaks a kingly oracle of a scepter and a star rising from within Israel who will crush the forehead of Moab. This king will do what the people of Israel could not do—obey the Lord and conquer their enemies. A future is approaching where the promises of a beautiful house full of the family of Israel will be realized. A King and a kingdom are coming, but somehow death, sacrifice, and a tree will also be involved.

Curses and Blessings

The kingdom terms in the Pentateuch are set not in terms of an abstract notion of sovereignty but in promises that sink deep into the physicality of life. God is the King of the cosmos, and he made his subjects to be rulers with him, but they failed. Pseudo-kingdoms arose after the fall. Cain's city continued the downward movement after Eden, and the Tower of Babel was the rebellious metropolis after the new creation with Noah.

With Abraham, kingdom hope was revived. God promised that Abraham's children would rule with a great multitude of people in a place God was preparing for them. A coming King would complete this kingdom mission, so the righteous seed of Abraham had to be preserved. Yahweh preserved his people by bringing them into and then out of Egypt. Once they were out, he gave them the law at Mount Sinai, instructing them through a covenant how they could ascend the mountain of the Lord. At the center of this plan stood the idea that someone must take their place.

Deuteronomy summarizes this story and renews God's covenant with the seed of Abraham as they prepare to enter the Land of Promise. After giving an overview of the history of Israel and renewing the terms of the covenant, Moses pronounces blessings upon those who obey the commandments and curses upon those who disobey. Deuteronomy also gives laws concerning future kings in the land

(17:14–20). All kings will be judged by this standard going forward. Central to Deuteronomy is the idea of life in the land. Peaceful and harmonious life in the land is a summary of what a gracious king brings. As James Hamilton says, "In many ways, Deuteronomy is the heart of the Old Testament. What comes before it leads up to this climactic moment of entering the land, and what comes after it is judged by the standards set in Deuteronomy."[10]

The importance of Deuteronomy at the close of the Pentateuch and its emphasis on land exemplify how the land and kingdom go hand in hand. The land Israel was about to possess is a gift from Yahweh, fulfilling the promise the Lord swore to their fathers (Deut. 6:23). It is painted in such a way as to remind Israel of the garden of Eden (Deut. 11:10–12).

To occupy the land, the people are required to keep the Lord's commands (Deut. 4:2, 6, 40; 5:1, 12, 29, 32; 6:2, etc.), but readers find that they would not do so completely. The fundamental issue is whether the people will acknowledge Yahweh as their King and choose to love God. Curses will come upon the people if they rejected their King. The blessings and curses are mainly centered on concrete realities.

Blessings (Deut. 28:1–14)	Curses (Deut. 28:15–68)
Blessed shall you be in the city and in the field.	Cursed shall you be in the city and in the field.
Blessed shall be the fruit of your womb.	Cursed be the fruit of your womb.
Blessed be your basket and kneading bowl.	Cursed shall be your basket and kneading bowl.
Blessed shall you be when you come in, and go out.	Cursed be you when you come in, and when you go out.
The Lord will defeat your enemies and bring blessings to your barns, wombs, livestock, and ground.	The Lord will strike you with disease, drought, enemies, death, boils, lack of crops, robbery.

---

10. James Hamilton, *God's Glory in Salvation through Judgment: A Biblical Theology* (Wheaton, IL: Crossway, 2010), 74.

These blessings and curses come in continuity of kingdom promises and warnings made to Abraham and Adam. Thus, it would be unwise to think of the kingdom in purely abstract terms. The kingdom promise concerns earthly things for the Israelites. As we will see, the New Testament does not subvert this theme; it confirms it.

The Kingdom in the Law

Kingship started before creation. The psalmist says, "The earth is the LORD's and the fullness thereof, / the world and those who dwell therein" (Ps. 24:1). He bases this on God's creating power: "For he has founded it upon the seas / and established it upon the rivers" (Ps. 24:2). Similarly, Psalm 93 asserts that the Lord reigns; his throne is established from of old; he is from everlasting (vv. 1–2). God is *the* great King over all the earth because he has created all things.[11] Theologians refer to this as God's universal kingdom or the cosmic dimension of his kingdom. He is the high King over the entire world. Kingship and kingdom begin with God, and the majority of the Bible focuses on his kingship manifested in and through creation.

The Pentateuch begins this story with God creating with words. He carved valleys into the earth through which the water flowed and caused the trees in the garden to grow tall and true. He made Adam and Eve kings and queens of this paradise. They were to be caretakers and rulers of creation, establishing God's kingdom on his behalf. Yet they decided to construct their own kingdom—without God; they chose the tree of death. Darkness, strife, and misery filled the earth. However, God had promised that despite Adam's sin, he would provide a successor who would not fail as Adam did. Therefore, God made covenants with people—with Noah, Abraham, and Moses. The kingdom hope that was *corrupted* with Adam and Eve was *revived*

---

11. Psalm 47:2.

with the promises to God's people. God would preserve this people because from them was coming a King who would lead his people into their place.

As the garden was situated on a mountain, so the Pentateuch closes with Moses ascending Mount Nebo and the Lord showing him all the land (Deut. 34:1). Yahweh affirms that this is the land he had promised to Abraham (Deut. 34:4). The silver thread of the land promise had not been dropped; Moses highlights it as a central theme. Moses dies on the mountain, unable to enter the land, but Joshua, the son of Nun, is spoken of as having a spirit of wisdom. Joshua will be the one to take the people into the land.

The kingdom hope that has been the goal of all creation is still making progress, because God fulfills his promises. Ultimately, the kingdom will be established through a new messianic King. John Sailhamer says, "One of the central issues in the message of the Pentateuch is the coming king and his eternal kingdom."[12] The Pentateuch highlights this messianic theme in major poems (Gen. 49:1; Num. 24:14; Deuteronomy 32). These poems characterize the central theme of the story. At the end of the Pentateuch, Moses's wooden staff points to a coming star, a scepter—one like Moses, Abraham, and Adam—but this one will be lifted up on a tree. He will inaugurate the kingdom, and the river will flow from the temple to water all the trees of the ground.

---

12. John H. Sailhamer, *The Meaning of the Pentateuch: Revelation, Composition and Interpretation* (Downers Grove, IL: IVP Academic, 2009), 37.

2

The Prophets

Foreshadowing the Kingdom

In his poem "Forgetfulness," American poet Billy Collins reflects on how our memories and thoughts pass into nothingness:

> The memories you used to harbor
> decided to retire to the southern hemisphere of the brain
> to a little fishing village where there are no phones.

He speaks of them

> floating down a dark mythological river
> whose name begins with an L as far as you can recall
> well on your own way to oblivion where you will join those.[1]

According to Collins, a fleeting nature envelops everything we think

---

1. Billy Collins, *Sailing Alone Around the Room: New and Selected Poems* (New York: Random House, 2002), 29.

and do, as if a friend is always quietly slipping out the door even as we welcome new acquaintances.

Remembering Promises

The picture of Yahweh presented in the Prophets is quite different. God has not forgotten any of the promises he had made to Abraham and his offspring. These guarantees were not "lurking in some obscure corner" of his mind;[2] rather, in the Prophets they occupy the center of the room and form the substructure of the rest of the conversation. In the Prophets we find the kingdom *foreshadowed* through the promise of an eternal throne. This promise is built on top of the previous guarantees. History does not just move on for the covenant God, he pushes it forward thorough the power of his Word as the saga strains toward its kingdom goal.

As the light begins to fade on the Pentateuch, the people of God are still seeking their inheritance of the land, or the place of the kingdom. Deuteronomy concludes with Moses looking out over the land on Mount Nebo. It is a tragic scene where the man who led Israel for so long is told he will not enter the land. However, there is hope, for this land is not the ultimate land God's people have yearned for. Yahweh will still give this land to Abraham's offspring. From this mountaintop the reader gazes over the land with Moses. What will happen once Israel enters the land? Will it be the home that the garden foreshadowed? Will God be with them and protect them? Will the kingdom be consummated? The Prophetic books begin to answer these questions.[3]

Readers find that as Israel enters the land, the kingdom has not been consummated, as they might expect; rather, the kingdom is *foreshadowed*. Readers do not witness the growth of a healthy tree

---

2. Ibid.

3. As noted earlier, I am following the Hebrew order. Therefore, the Prophets include Joshua, Judges, Samuel, Kings, Isaiah, Jeremiah, Ezekiel, and the twelve Minor Prophets.

under which the nations will gather; instead, the branches show signs of disease and decay. Growth has again been stunted by the sin of the people. There are still glimmers of hope as righteous branches spring up, but the tree is not maturing as expected. The people and their kings end up disobeying the laws of their true King and are sent into exile.

So while the land was gifted to God's people, and they appointed kings, things are still not right. Isaiah promises that out of this struggling tree a shoot will sprout and a new city will be established to which the nations will stream. This city will be more glorious than they ever imagined. Hope is not lost.

Land, Judges, and Kings

Joshua recounts the story of the people entering their land. It begins with Israel at the doorstep and concludes with them established in Canaan. The land is a symbol for the new creation, and the Israelites are to cross over the water (the Jordan River) to enter into the land (Josh. 1:2–3). As the Israelites tread the Jordan, we are reminded of the Holy Spirit brooding over the water in Genesis, bringing order out of chaos. The people of Israel are the means by which God acts upon his creation, and the promise of the land is a foretaste of what God intends for the whole creation. Kingdom promises concern all of life: material, physical, and spiritual. To spiritualize these promises is to flatten the kingdom tree into a cardboard cutout when it is actually a living organism.

Joshua emphasizes that while God acts through his people, the people are entirely dependent upon the Lord for success. It is God who brings them into their kingdom through the Jordan. The angel of the Lord appears to Joshua with a sword in his hand (Josh. 5:13–15), and the Israelites march around Jericho for seven days after which God collapses its walls (Josh. 6:2–3).

All these events signify that the Lord is the one fighting for them. God builds his kingdom. And God is concerned not just with Israel. Joshua 6–12 details the battles with the Canaanites, but the likes of Rahab (the Canaanite) and the Gibeonites find themselves in a pact with the people of God. There are already hints that the promises to Israel are intended for more than Israel. At the end of the invasion, a summary is given: "Joshua took the whole land, according to all that the LORD had spoken to Moses. And Joshua gave it for an inheritance to Israel according to their tribal allotments" (Josh. 11:23).

But what was the purpose of life in the land? A few purposes rise to the surface. Most fundamentally, it was to be the home of God's people where they could commune with God. Through this stability, they would also be a light to the nations. The kingdom promises concern an upward (God), inward (communal and personal), and outward (missional) dimension. Israel had to realize that they could be a light to the nations only if they lived in a right relationship with God and with one another.[4]

A problem remains though; the tree is diseased at the root and is thus being destroyed from the inside. The stain of sin shoots through Israel's branches just as it does the rest of the nations. They don't obey God's word (Judges 1), and after Joshua dies, the people follow the "gods" and the kings of Canaan. Israel divides its loyalty between Baal the fertility god and the King of the universe, who owns the cattle on a thousand hills. Israel falls into a cycle of turning from God, experiencing oppression, and crying out, and then God providing a new deliverer. God is gracious to them despite their sin. Each judge is a picture of the deliverer to come who will rescue people by his power and restore the land.

---

4. It is frustrating how some will emphasize one of these aspects over the other. Popular in some circles today is to emphasize the main purpose as being a light to the nations. While this is true, the foundation of being a light to the nations is a relationship with God.

One of the reasons given in the book of Judges for Israel's rapid decline into sin is that "in those days there was no king in Israel. Everyone did what was right in his own eyes" (Judg. 21:25). Although Israel already had a divine King, they needed a leader who would embody the law of the Lord, rescue them from their enemies, and lead the people in righteous living (Deut. 17:18–20). The desire for a king was not wrong, for God was making them into a great nation; the problem was that they wanted a king like the other nations' (1 Sam. 8:4–22).

Saul is thus set up by Samuel (the last judge of Israel) as the first king of Israel. But things do not go as planned. Saul does not follow the law of the Lord, and God instructs Samuel to begin looking for another king to bring peace. He anoints David, of the tribe of Judah, a young man from Bethlehem, and the Spirit comes upon David and departs from Saul.[5] Like Adam and Abraham, David turns out to be a central figure throughout the rest of the story.

After the death of Saul, David rules faithfully over the nation and establishes the people in their home by defeating their enemies. This king wields the sword for the good and safety of his people. David also brings the ark of the covenant to Jerusalem and desires to build a home for the Lord. But the prophet Nathan tells David that David's son will build the Lord's house. However, the Lord is so pleased with David that he establishes a covenant with him and promises to (1) make David's name great, (2) provide a place for the people of Israel where God will "plant" them so they will be secure, (3) give them rest from their enemies, and (4) establish David's dynasty forever.

The promises to Abraham echo through the first three promises to David, but the fourth is new: David's dynasty will last forever. The kingdom David establishes foreshadows the kingdom waiting to be

---

5. Here an important link emerges between the role of the Spirit and the King of Israel, which the New Testament will pick up.

inaugurated in the New Testament. As Dempster notes, "From this one location in world *geography* and this one location in world *genealogy* will flow blessing to the entire world and its inhabitants. This is the theme that reverberates throughout the rest of the Bible."[6] David was the king, the one to whom all other kings throughout the history of Israel will be compared. The true promised King will be one of David's children. God has not forgotten his promises to Abraham.

Concepts	Power	People	Place
Abraham is promised . . .	a great nation	seed/children	land
David is promised . . .	a great name	rest from enemies	rest from enemies
	a forever dynasty (new promise)		

Solomon, David's son, rules as king once David dies, and he builds the house of the Lord, as Nathan had promised. Was Solomon the promised one? No, the downward spiral that we saw in Genesis has begun again. Solomon takes many foreign wives and allows the worship of rival gods, and his heart is led astray. His actions were forbidden, according to Deuteronomy. Solomon also displeases God by amassing large amounts of money and building a big army with chariots and horses from Egypt. Idolatry begins to pollute Israel because the king is not leading the people as he ought. The result of this failed king is a divided people.

After Solomon's death, the kingdom is split in two. The land God had promised is torn apart by the sin of the king. Judah, the southern kingdom, continues with the Davidic throne, while the northern kingdom, Israel, appoints its own new dynasty. At this point, the prophets begin to play a large role. They call Israel and their kings to repentance, warn of coming judgment, and promise hope if the peo-

---

6. Stephen Dempster, *Dominion and Dynasty: A Theology of the Hebrew Bible*, New Studies in Biblical Theology (Downers Grove, IL: IVP Academic, 2003), 142.

ple return to the law of the Lord. But the divided kingdom continues to slide toward disaster, and ultimately foreign nations conquer the people and exile them from their land. The people of God are split, the land is ravaged, and the people no longer have a ruler. The books of the Kings thus look back on the rise and decline of the monarchy, explaining how exile came about.[7]

Joshua ends with the people dwelling in Canaan, but the books of the Kings end with exile! The promises of the kingdom are in disarray. As in Genesis, the people have collapsed under the weight of the temptation to run after other gods and have been exiled from their land. And they have no king. It seems that the Serpent's kingdom is winning. Who will rescue them? Will Yahweh continue to be a faithful King and appoint a ruler for them, or has God's kingdom vision evaporated because of the sin of his people?

Warnings and Visions

The Prophetic Books seek to answer those questions. The writing prophets look through the kingdom lens as they call the people of Yahweh back to the covenant by both warnings and promising visions of a future kingdom that will be greater than David's. If the people were to continue in sin, rival kingdoms would overthrow them, but inherent in the prophets' message is that even though the people prove faithless, God will send a faithful one.

The King as Judge and Comforter

The image of a king governs the entire book of Isaiah.[8] One day, God will send a future King from the line of David (power), who will lead

---

7. Kings is different from Chronicles, for Chronicles looks further back to the promises to Adam and his purposes for the entire creation. This is why the Hebrew Scriptures end with Chronicles, because it is an *inclusio* to the book of Genesis.

8. See Andrew Abernethy, *The Book of Isaiah and God's Kingdom: A Thematic-Theological Approach* (Downers Grove, IL: IVP Academic, 2016).

Israel in obedience to the covenant (people), and this blessing will go to the whole world (place). With Isaiah, we lift up our eyes to Yahweh the King in chapter 6, a vision that casts a shadow over the entire book. Isaiah sees the Lord sitting high on his throne (Isa. 6:1).

Sitting on a throne connotes royal power, but in Isaiah's context the power is defined specifically as authority in judgment. A few indicators in the text confirm this. First, the throne on which God sits is a place where judgment is executed. Second, the seraphim surrounding the throne are snakelike figures who symbolize coming destruction. "Since punishment accompanies every mention of the seraphim in the OT, this vision of seraphim would send shivers down one's spine: judgement is looming."[9] Third, the holiness of the Lord demands purging. A coal is given to Isaiah to cleanse his lips, and smoke fills the temple. The King is about to break forth in divine and purifying judgment, and the larger context of chapters 1–39 bears this out. Good kings not only rescue their people but mete out justice.

The King not only brings judgment but also comfort to his people. The latter half of the book (Isaiah 40–66) is a message of comfort for those who obey his voice, as the train of his robe contains not only threads of judgment but strands of tenderness. He speaks comfort to his people (Isa. 40:1–2), and he brings salvation to his people who follow him:

> Thus says the LORD:
>   "Keep justice, and do righteousness
> for soon my salvation will come,
>   and my righteousness be revealed." (Isa. 56:1)

He comes to revive the spirit of the lowly and to revive the heart of the oppressed (Isa. 57:15). He looks favorably on the one who is

---

9. Ibid., 17.

humble and submissive in spirit and trembles at his word (Isa. 66:1). So while God is presented as Judge, he is also portrayed as the King who is tender in heart. But where does this latter hope stem from? Has the King merely changed his mind?

Hope is manifested through a coming leader who is presented from three complimentary perspectives.[10] The first image, given in Isaiah 1–39, is of a *Davidic ruler*. He will promote justice and righteousness and be the light to the nations (Isa. 9:2); upon his shoulders the government will sit, and his dominion will be vast (Isa. 9:6–7). He is the shoot growing from the stump of Jesse upon whom the Spirit will rest (Isa. 11:1–10). Comfort comes through this Davidic figure.

But comfort also comes through a second figure, the servant of the Lord (Isaiah 40–55). The servant brings salvation, raises up the tribes of Jacob, and restores the protected ones of Israel (Isa. 49:1–7). He will be lifted up, although many will be appalled by him (Isa. 52:13–15). He will bring consolation by bearing pain, sickness, and affliction, and through him the nation will be healed (Isa. 53:1–12). Finally, comfort will come through the Spirit-anointed messenger of God. The messenger will announce good news to the poor, heal, and proclaim liberty to the captives (Isa. 61:1–3).

Isaiah presents a picture of God the King. God is the Judge, but he is also the tender King to his people because of this Davidic servant messenger who brings restoration, the new exodus, the new creation, and the new Zion. While God's reign is everywhere, and the earth is his footstool (Isa. 66:1), the epicenter of his reign will be in Zion from which he will bless all nations.

The kingdom God brings is *through* power and a person, and *for* a place. He will create a new heaven and a new earth and Jerusalem to be a joy (Isa. 65:17–18). In the New Jerusalem, there will be no

---

10. I am reliant on Abernethy here for the three images. Ibid., 11.

crying (Isa. 65:19), no death (Isa. 65:20), no governmental systems of oppression (Isa. 65:21–22), and no conflict (Isa. 65:25)—all because of this coming Davidic servant messenger.

Uprooting and Planting

Like Isaiah's prophecies, Jeremiah's prophecies gather under the banner of the kingdom. Jeremiah's message and mission are explained in chapter 1 where Yahweh says he has set him over nations and kingdoms. The prophets were spokesmen to earthly kingdoms from the heavenly King. And how was Jeremiah's task designated? He will "pluck up and . . . break down, / . . . destroy and . . . overthrow, / . . . build and . . . plant" (Jer. 1:10). Unsurprisingly, the imagery is that of a tree. Jeremiah proclaims the uprooting of Israel for the breaking of the old covenant but promises that God will plant them once again through a new covenant and a new David.

Jeremiah's writing begins before the exile, but he lives through the exile to Babylon, watching with horror as his words come true. In Jeremiah 1–24 he accuses and warns Israel that they have not kept the covenant. The second half of the book pronounces judgment on Israel (chaps. 26–45) and on the nations (chaps. 46–51). However, grace remains for both, because the "LORD of hosts" (think kingly imagery) will break the yokes off their necks, and burst their bonds (Jer. 30:8).

Kings rescue their people, and Jeremiah promises that the King will gather them (Jer. 31:8) and restore their fortunes (Jer. 31:23), and they will dwell together (Jer. 31:24). The language with which Jeremiah was commissioned occurs again as Yahweh reminds us that he is acting through his prophets to watch over Israel as he uproots and breaks down. He will also watch over them to build and to plant (Jer. 31:28). He will make a new covenant with them—one that fulfills what Moses spoke about so many years before, at the end of Deuteronomy.

The book of Jeremiah concludes as his words of judgment are enacted. The people of Israel are destroyed and carried into exile (chap. 52). But glimmers of hope still shine through. Jeremiah promises that the kingdom of Babylon, raging against God's anointed nation, will be destroyed (chaps. 50–51). The city of Babylon harkens back both geographically and symbolically to the first city to defy the God of heaven (see Genesis 11). The kingdom of the Serpent wars against the kingdom of God as it has done since the beginning, but Yahweh will still plant his tree in the center of the earth and call all nations to himself. He is protecting this line of Judah, the seed of David, even while his people are in exile.

Return from Exile

Ezekiel, like Isaiah and Jeremiah, has visions of the coming kingdom, but his focus is on the presence of the King and the return from exile through the servant of David. Ezekiel sees a vision of the Lord sitting on a throne, but the throne has wheels that show that the glory of the Lord has departed from Jerusalem (Ezekiel 10).[11] Ezekiel sees the presence of the King leaving on these wheels because the people have not obeyed the covenant of their true King.

Judgment will fall on Israel (Ezekiel 12–24) and on the nations (Ezekiel 25–32) and then finally on Jerusalem (Ezekiel 33). The climax of this judgment is on the city of Jerusalem, where "the waste places shall fall by the sword" and the people will be devoured by beasts (Ezek. 33:27). Judgment falls on both the people and the land.

While condemning the people, Ezekiel also promises that the exile is not ultimately the end. God will "gather" the people and "assemble" them and give them back their land (Ezek. 11:17). He will give them a new heart and a new spirit, and they will walk in the law

---

11. Here an important theme is picked up that I have not talked much about: presence.

of the King again, and God will dwell with them (Ezek. 11:19–20). The second half of the book gives hope for Israel (Ezekiel 34–37), for all nations (Ezekiel 38–39), and for all of creation (Ezekiel 40–48).

This hope for the people in their place comes only through the new Shepherd King of the line of David (Ezek. 34:23), who will remake their land. The people will dwell securely, and the Shepherd King will provide them renewed plantations (Ezek. 34:39–40).

> My servant David shall be king over them, and they shall all have one shepherd. They shall walk in my rules and be careful to obey my statutes. They shall dwell in the land that I gave to my servant Jacob, where your fathers lived. They and their children and their children's children shall dwell there forever, and David my servant shall be their prince forever. I will make a covenant of peace with them. It shall be an everlasting covenant with them. And I will set them in their land and multiply them, and will set my sanctuary in their midst forevermore. My dwelling place shall be with them, and I will be their God, and they shall be my people. (Ezek. 37:24–27)

Ezekiel ends with the temple (a picture of all creation). He promises that a temple will be rebuilt, which will be larger and much better than Solomon's. The throne chariot enters the temple, signifying the King's presence returning to his people and establishing them in their place. The river then flows out of the temple and transforms the Dead Sea into a garden city named "The LORD is There" (Ezek. 48:35). God's kingly presence transforms the people and their place into a good and safe kingdom.

Isaiah, Jeremiah, and Ezekiel record the words of Yahweh to the kingdoms of the earth and to the kingdom of Israel. To understand these words, one needs to understand the Torah. With these prophetic words, kingdoms are uprooted and built up. Yahweh has raised up foreign kingdoms to exile the people of Abraham because of their sin. But the judgment of God will also fall on these rival kingdoms. Yahweh has not turned his back on his people. Israel is still his chosen people, and one from their tribe will rescue them. A Davidic servant messenger will lead them back.

Each prophet speaks of a transformed people and a renewed place. A new covenant will be made; the presence of God will return to the land but only through a coming King. Although exile still looms like an ominous rain cloud, the shoot from the tree will spring up, break through the clouds, and be seen from the four corners of the earth.

The Day of the Lord

Like the Major Prophets (Isaiah, Jeremiah, and Ezekiel), the twelve Minor Prophets announce judgment and promise restoration.[12] They ground their message in obedience or disobedience to the covenant, emphasizing concrete blessings or curses and announcing that the day of the Lord is coming. The Minor Prophets lean on the history of Israel and point to a coming kingdom.

The Minor Prophets are framed by references to the covenant conveyed through familial imagery.[13] The first book, Hosea, portrays Israel as God's wife. Hosea's children are named "No Mercy" and "Not My People"—a harsh message from God to Israel (Hos. 1:8–9). Yet these names will be changed to "children of the living God" (Hos. 1:10). The last book of the twelve, Malachi, speaks about love (Mal.

---

12. The Minor Prophets include Hosea, Joel, Amos, Obadiah, Jonah, Micah, Nahum, Habakkuk, Zephaniah, Haggai, Zechariah, and Malachi.

13. See John D. W. Watts, "A Frame for the Book of the Twelve: Hosea 1–3 and Malachi," in *Reading and Hearing the Book of the Twelve*, Society of Biblical Literature Symposium Series 15 (Atlanta, GA: Society of Biblical Literature, 2000), 209–17.

1:2) and the relationship between Yahweh and Jacob and Esau. The crisis in the relationship is like that between son and father (Mal. 1:6): "A son honors his father, and a servant his master. If then I am a father, where is my honor?" Malachi continues in 2:10: "Have we not all one Father? Has not one God created us? Why then are we faithless to one another, profaning the covenant of our fathers?"

Why do the Minor Prophets speak in these intimate, relational terms? And what are the implications for our understanding of the kingdom? God refers to Israel as his son in Exodus, and although the language of fatherhood is rare in the Old Testament, it does occur in Deuteronomy 32:6, where Moses calls Yahweh the father of the nation of Israel. Like the rest of the prophets, the twelve Minor Prophets dwell in the shadow of the Torah, more specifically the end of Deuteronomy. Moses foretold:

> When all these things come upon you, the blessing and the curse, . . . and you call them to mind . . . and return to the LORD your God, . . . then the LORD your God will restore your fortunes and have mercy on you. (Deut. 30:1–3)

That is an expression of hope *through* judgment. The curses must come first, and then their hearts will be moved. The curses will be turned to blessings if they walk in obedience to their King and Father. The domestic language that frames the Minor Prophets thus pushes readers back to the idea of covenant found in the Torah. As Tom Schreiner says, "virtually everything said about the Twelve could fit under the category of covenant."[14] According to the Minor Prophets (and the rest of the Scriptures), the kingdom will arise through the covenant.

Second, the Minor Prophets emphasize the concrete blessings

---

14. Thomas R. Schreiner, *The King in His Beauty: A Biblical Theology of the Old and New Testaments* (Grand Rapids, MI: Baker Academic, 2013), 397.

and curses of this covenantal relationship. Judgment is not abstract but meted out in the form of the exile. Restoration, in the same way, includes establishing the nation in their land. Reinstatement will come not through the might or righteousness of the people but through the faithfulness of God to his covenant with Abraham. This restoration is portrayed as bringing the people back to their land:

> Though I scattered them among the nations,
>> yet in far countries they shall remember me,
>> and with their children they shall live and return.
> I will bring them home from the land of Egypt,
>> and gather them from Assyria,
> and I will bring them to the land of Gilead and to Lebanon,
>> till there is no room for them. (Zech. 10:9–10)

The kingdom blessings concern a return from exile and repossession of the land. They envision renewed prosperity in terms of agricultural bounty and an increase of livestock and people.

These blessings are notably physical, embodied, and material. The expectation of the people of Israel was not an ethereal or abstract hope but one grounded in the physical realities of life. The promises to Adam, Abraham, and David run through the Minor Prophets, emphasizing seed, land, rest, a king, worldwide blessing, and God's presence with his people. These should all be seen under the canopy of the kingdom of God. If we erase the spatial or person-centered aspects of the kingdom from our definition, then we might as well erase the twelve Minor Prophets from the Scriptures.

A final theme that appears repeatedly in the Minor Prophets is the "day of the Lord." Joel especially emphasizes this idea (Joel 1:15; 2:1–2, 31; 3:14), but Amos (Amos 5:18), Obadiah (Obad. 15), Zephaniah (Zeph. 1:7–10, 14–18), and Malachi (Mal. 4:5) all mention it as well. Many of the prophets shorten it to simply "that day" or associate it with specific kingdom imagery.[15] The day of the Lord refers to when the Lord will arrive to judge the foreign nations and deliver his people. Such deliverance is the king's job. He is to use his power to overthrow nations, deliver his people, and win back their land. For the Minor Prophets, the hope was future oriented. They envisioned the day when the Lord their King would assert his authority over the whole world (Zechariah 12–14; Mal. 4:1–6).

The Minor Prophets continue the themes of judgment and hope for the people of Israel. Like the Major Prophets, they too focus on the kingdom hope that arrives through covenant. They prophesy of God as Father, the day of the Lord, and the physical blessings associated with the kingdom. As they look back to the covenant God made with Israel's forefathers, they also look forward to a new covenant and a new creation. Although the term *kingdom* occurs only six times in the Minor Prophets (Hos. 1:4; Amos 6:2; 7:13; 9:8; Obad. 21; Nah. 3:5), this covenantal concept is the backdrop through which all their writings cohere.[16]

The Kingdom in the Prophets

In the Prophetic Literature, the kingdom is foreshadowed. The section starts with such hope. The people stand on the edge of their land and catch a glimpse of a life of abundance and flourishing. God even gives them a king after his own heart, but the nation continually chooses to eat fruit from diseased trees. So God gives them over to their desires. Foreign kingdoms conquer them, and the people of God go into exile.

The prophets both warn of this impending judgment and offer

---

15. Hos. 1:5; 2:16, 18, 21; 5:9; 7:5; 9:5; Joel 3:18; Amos 1:14; 3:14; 6:3; 8:3, 9, 13; Obad. 8, 11 13, 14; Mic. 2:4; 4:6; 7:4, 12; Hab. 3:16; Zeph. 2:2–3; 3:8, 11, 16; Hag. 2:23; Zech. 2:11; 3:10; 9:16; 12:3–11; 13:1–4; 14:1–20; Mal. 3:2, 17; 4:1–5.

16. In Amos 6:2 there is parallelism that links kingdom to territory. "Are you better than these kingdoms? / Or is their territory greater than your territory?"

hope. God sits as King in Isaiah's prophecy, with both judgment and comfort flowing from the train of his robe. Jeremiah lives through the exile and promises a new covenant, and Ezekiel tells of a new exodus when the people will rebuild their temple. In the Major Prophets, restoration is viewed in tangible terms. The Minor Prophets in a similar fashion tell of coming wrath but also of blessings. In the day of the Lord, God will reestablish his people. Both Major and Minor Prophets call the people back to the covenant stipulations that their true King gave them on Mount Sinai.

Malachi concludes the Prophetic Books by speaking about the coming day of the Lord (Mal. 4:1–6). Malachi says that "the day is coming" when those who fear the Lord will be healed and those who do not will be tread like ashes under his feet. He commands them to remember the Law of Moses, promising that the Lord will send a prophet before the day comes. This prophet will turn the hearts of the people lest the Lord strike the land with utter destruction. Throughout the Prophets, there are hints that utter destruction can be forestalled only by a good king. But what will this king do?

Isaiah speaks of this one as the suffering servant; Ezekiel speaks of him as a shepherd; Jeremiah as a King. All of them paint him as one who will bring them out of exile. The leader they are waiting for will establish their tree as the tallest. The Writings will speak in greater detail of the work of the good King, who will plant his people by streams of living water.

3

The Writings

Life in the Kingdom

Poetry has a musical quality. It molds, twists, and orders words to enlighten gradually. Emily Dickinson once said,

> Tell all the truth but tell it slant—
> Success in Circuit lies
> Too bright for our infirm Delight.[1]

She uses the metaphor of light as a symbol for truth. Light can be glaring and drive people away, or it can be soft and gather attention. Dickinson's point is that truth can be communicated in different ways; sometimes an altered angle is more effective than direct sunshine.

---

1 Emily Dickinson, *The Pocket Emily Dickinson*, ed. Brenda Hillman (Boston: Shambhala, 2009), 137.

Light and Truth

In a similar way, the Writings have the ability to speak in a more nuanced way, providing different perspectives through both poetry and narrative.[2] As Dickinson might say, the Writings present the kingdom *slant*. They reflect on what "kingdom life" looks like through proverbs, songs, laments, stories, and more history. Either the people will follow God's wise King and live, or they will reject the commands of the King and die. The theme of life and death stretches back to the garden in Genesis, where Adam faced a choice between—of all things—two trees. The Writings, in a similar way, cast the choice between wisdom and folly, a choice between life and death.

For too long the Writings have been relegated to a footnote when it comes to the kingdom story. Yet three realities push against this tendency. First, many of these writings come from the kings of Israel, written to the people (Israel) of God the King. Second, the Wisdom Literature (a part of the Writings) is an outworking of the commands of the Creator King. Third, the aim of this literature is to return Israel to their God and to establish the people in their place (the land). If the kingdom concerns people and place alongside power, then the Writings fit comfortably under the banner of the kingdom. The king not only rescues his people and provides security in the land, but he also teaches them how to live a full life in that land.

The ideal king was to lead the nation in a flourishing life full of wisdom, knowledge, and the fear of the Lord. If the prophets zoom in on the covenant stipulations, then the Writings examine *life in the kingdom*. We have charted how the kingdom was *established* with Adam and Eve as king and queen, *corrupted* through the rival kingdom of the Serpent and his children, *revived* through the promises to Abra-

---

2. The Writings in the Hebrew ordering include Psalms, Job, Proverbs, Ruth, Song of Solomon, Ecclesiastes, Lamentations, Esther, Daniel, Ezra, Nehemiah, and Chronicles. See the chart on pp. 25–26 for an overview of the comparison of the English and Hebrew listing.

ham, and *foreshadowed* in the Davidic kingdom. This chapter rounds out the Old Testament, giving a poetic picture of life in the kingdom.

Law	Reviving hope in the kingdom
Prophets	Foreshadowing the kingdom
Writings	**Life in the kingdom**

Wisdom Literature and the Good Life

The Wisdom Books look to individuals and kings who embody the good life by fearing the Lord, acquiring wisdom and following the Torah, and suffering righteously. This instruction comes mainly in the form of proverbs, poetry, laments, and songs. Each piece of the Wisdom Literature teaches the citizens of the kingdom to walk in the ways of the Torah, like their virtuous king, so they can be established in their land. The Wisdom Literature focuses on the king (power), the Torah (law for people), and the land (place). Although each writer (and many of them kings) who wrote these words ultimately failed in their tasks, their writings lean forward to a day when a new King will be the people's wisdom and righteousness. If the kingdom is the tree, then the Wisdom Literature explains how leaves of the tree can blossom and not wither and perish.

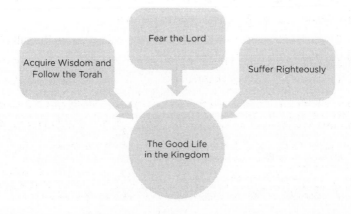

The Wisdom Literature reflects on the nature of this "good life" under the ideal king. How does the Wisdom Literature describe it? Proverbs casts the obtainment of the good life as a choice between wisdom and foolishness—a decision between life and death. Not surprisingly, life is presented as dwelling in the land and having a physical blessing. In Proverbs the wise will retain the land (Prov. 2:21–22). The wicked will be uprooted from the land (Prov. 10:30). "By justice a king builds up the land, / but he who exacts gifts tears it down" (Prov. 29:4). The good life is at least partially defined as living in the land. The Wisdom Literature aims at the good life in contrast to the way of death, as warned about in Deuteronomy.

Proverbs and Psalms also refer to the good life through the language of blessing. Noting the language of blessing, readers should think back to the kingdom promises made to Abraham. According to Proverbs, blessed ones are those who find wisdom and live prudently (e.g., Prov. 3:13; 8:32, 34; 14:21; 29:18). The Psalms begin, "Blessed is the man / who walks not in the counsel of the wicked . . . but his delight is in the law of the LORD" (Ps. 1:1–2). Delighting in the law of the Lord echoes what the king is to do according to Deuteronomy. The one who delights in the law becomes a well-watered tree, an embodiment of the kingdom under which the nation can find rest.

Psalm 2 then recounts how this prosperous tree (this blessed one of Psalm 1) stands opposed to the kings of the earth. The Lord supports his Anointed One and laughs at those who mock his chosen King (Ps. 2:4). While the wicked sit and scoff in Psalm 1, the Lord of heaven sits and laughs back at them in Psalm 2. This psalm depicts the war that continues between the kingdoms of the earth (the wicked) and the kingdom of heaven (the righteous). The Lord *has* established his tree, and it will never be moved. His King will conquer (Ps. 2:6–9). As Psalm 1 begins with "blessed," so Psalm 2 ends with, "Blessed are all who take refuge in [the Lord's king]" (v. 12).

Thus, the Wisdom Literature focuses on what it means to flourish, to be blessed, to prosper—to live this good life. Death is avoided and kingdom life is attained in three ways: (1) acquiring wisdom and following the Torah, (2) fearing the Lord, and (3) submitting to suffering. If Israel is to grow into a strong cedar, they must rest beneath the shade of God, who is their King, and the one he has appointed to lead them. The goal of the Wisdom Literature is to lead the people of Israel toward a life of flourishing.

Acquire Wisdom and Follow the Torah

To live the good life, one must acquire wisdom and follow the Torah. This is because God is King over all creation (and therefore all wisdom flows from him), and he has set up his king who is instructed to follow the Torah. Throughout the Scriptures wisdom and Torah are interlocked. Deuteronomy 4:6 speaks of the Torah as Israel's wisdom and understanding before the nations (see Prov. 1:2). In Psalms, the Torah is sweeter than honey (Ps. 119:103), and in Proverbs, Solomon calls his teaching "wisdom" (Prov. 4:11; 5:1; 8:1; 10:31; 19:20). The Torah is also connected to wisdom in Ezra, which mentions the "Law of your God, which is in your hand" (Ezra 7:14). Later in the address, Ezra says, "according to the wisdom of your God that is in your hand" (v. 25).[3]

Both kings (and other individuals) instruct people on how to live the blessed life. This includes reflection both on the Torah and on what it means to live life more generally, because God is King over all creation (Job; Ecclesiastes). Israel's kings make appearances throughout the poetic section of the Hebrew Scriptures. Many of the psalms were composed by David; Ecclesiastes begins, "The . . . son of David, king in Jerusalem" (Eccles. 1:1); Song of Solomon has

---

3. Jonathan Akin, "A Theology of Future Hope in the Book of Proverbs," PhD diss., The Southern Baptist Theological Seminary (2012), 88–89.

many references to Solomon; Proverbs similarly says, "The son of David, king of Israel" (Prov. 1:1). "The wisdom literature is thus a result of the good king obeying the commands of Deuteronomy 6 and 17 and passing them onto the crown prince or vice-regents of his kingdom."[4] Solomon casts his proverbs as instructions from a father to a son, training him to be the ideal king who establishes David's forever dynasty. The good king will rule in wisdom and righteousness *by obeying* the Torah. He is to decree laws (Prov. 16:10), execute justice (Prov. 31:8–9), and pour out wrath on evil-doers (Prov. 16:14). Obeying or disobeying will result in life or death for the king and the whole nation. As the king goes, so goes the nation.

But this wisdom is also presented through the lens of living full of wisdom because God is the King of creation. Ecclesiastes reflects on what it means to live on the earth. Job submits that despite his lack of knowledge, God is still King of creation. The Song of Solomon examines the nature of a marriage relationship, and Proverbs reflects on the parent-child relationship. Lamentations examines what it looks like to weep. In Proverbs, the tree of life image is once again picked up as an image of life in the kingdom:

> She is a tree of life to those who lay hold of her;
> > those who hold her fast are called blessed. (Prov. 3:18)

> The fruit of the righteous is a tree of life,
> > and whoever captures souls is wise. (Prov. 11:30)

Through the leadership of the king and these other individuals, the people are planted as oaks of righteousness in their land. The way to the land is by mimicking the good king in wisdom and meditating, obeying, and following the Torah.

---

4. Ibid., 94.

The Fear of the Lord

The good king leads the people in the good life by embodying the Torah, and he teaches his crown prince to do the same. Two other specific ways of living the good life come to the surface in the Wisdom Literature: fearing the Lord and suffering. The authors of Ecclesiastes and Proverbs argue that the good life's source is the fear of the Lord. Ecclesiastes presents the critic (Eccles. 1:3–12:7). He argues that life is meaningless because of the fleeting nature of time (Eccles. 1:3–11), the fact that we all die (Eccles. 11:7–12:7), and the random nature of life. The cynical critic argues that you can't control anything. Life is unclear, confusing, and uncontrollable. The author responds that it is right to live in fear of the Lord and keep his commandments: "The end of the matter; all has been heard. Fear God and keep his commandments, for this is the whole duty of man" (Eccles. 12:13).

The call is not to ignore the randomness of life, or the nature of time, or the reality of death, but to stop trying to control these things; rather, trust and obey. Wisdom is found not where the critic searched but in the simple fear of the Lord. In many ways, wisdom is defined as fearing the Lord.

Proverbs also speaks about the fear of the Lord as the way to the good life. The fear of the Lord is depicted as the beginning of wisdom (Prov. 1:7; 9:10), as prolonging life (Prov. 10:27), and as the fountain of life (Prov. 14:27). The fear of the Lord is a reverential awe for Yahweh. As Waltke notes, it is both the cause and the effect; revering the Lord enables one to follow the Torah, and by following the law one fears the Lord.[5] In both Ecclesiastes and Proverbs, the fear of the Lord is connected to the Torah. The king must embody the Torah and fear the Lord so the people can live safely in their kingdom.

---

5. Bruce Waltke, "The Book of Proverbs and Old Testament Theology," *Bibliotheca Sacra* 136 (October 1979): 313.

Righteous Suffering

By fearing the Lord and following the king, the people will enjoy the good life, but the path to the kingdom is paradoxically also a road of suffering. This suffering many times comes at the hands of kingdoms opposed to the kingdom of God. Job, Psalms, and Lamentations all concern the suffering of God's people and point to one who will suffer on behalf of Israel. To live, flourish, and experience spring, the tree must first submit to the death of winter.

Consider Job. His friends assume that his suffering stems from some fault in his life, but he maintains that he is innocent. The assumption of both Job and his friends is that righteous living will result in a life without suffering. But Yahweh appears to Job in the whirlwind and affirms that his ways are beyond human comprehension. Job's mouth is shut in silence, and with him we learn that righteousness and suffering are not opposing forces but two sides of the same coin.

The psalms also embody this theme especially as applied to David, *the* righteous sufferer (see Psalms 7; 22; 69; 109). In these psalms, David the king suffers and points to the nature of the coming King, who will also suffer. In Psalm 73 Asaph speaks of the temptation of the righteous to envy the prosperity of the arrogant wicked (v. 3). In Psalm 22 David cries out to God for forsaking him (v. 1) and recounts how evildoers encompass him and pierce his feet (v. 16). David also says that many rise against him (Ps. 3:1); all day his enemies taunt him and curse his name (Ps. 102:8). Yet David cries out for help and calls on the Lord his King to deliver him.

Lamentations is another example of where the people of God cry out in anguish to God because of their exile. The lament begins with the lonely city (Lam. 1:1) and personifies it as a widow. The suffering here is different from that seen in some of the psalms and in Job because this suffering comes from Jerusalem's sin (Lam. 1:8). "Her uncleanness was in her skirts; / she took no thought of her future; / therefore her fall is terrible" (Lam. 1:9). The author speaks of the Lord being in the right because his people rebelled against his word (Lam. 1:18). Yet in the center of the book, there is hope, for the Lord is good to those who wait for him, "who wait . . . for the salvation of the LORD" (Lam. 3:24–26). The kingdom will advance through waiting on the Lord in the midst of suffering.

Ruth: A New King Is Coming

Crammed in the middle of the Wisdom Literature, based on the ordering of the Hebrew Scriptures, is a short narrative about two women: Ruth and Naomi. In one sense, it's an odd place for the book of Ruth. In terms of chronology, Ruth comes long before David's kingship. In terms of the canonical ordering of the Hebrew Scriptures, Ruth occurs long after the kingdom had split and the people had gone into exile. But perhaps the placement among the Writings makes sense.[6]

Each of the kings featured in the Wisdom Literature had failed to bring about an eternal state of the good life, but Ruth reminds the people that God will bring his rescuer King. In Ruth the people of Yahweh find themselves away from their home, living in Moab (Ruth 1:1). In exile many of them die, but a few return to find a compassionate redeemer. Through marriage to this redeemer a son, Obed, is born to Naomi through Ruth. "He was the father of Jesse, the father of David" (Ruth 4:17).

In the midst of hardship, in the middle of life without hope, this little narrative reminds Israel that God has not abandoned his people. Just as David came in an unexpected way through the line of

---

6. The placement of Ruth after Proverbs is also motivated by the fact that she is the only woman in the Bible explicitly designated as the "woman of valor" described in Proverbs 31.

Ruth, so too a new King is coming who will light the pathway out of Moab, out of exile.

Summary: Waiting for the King

The Wisdom Literature looks forward to the ideal king who embodies the Torah and teaches his people how to live the good life in the land of the Lord. It also speaks of those who fear God because he is the Creator of all things and therefore the King. The people are to keep the covenant because God is King. If they do, they will flourish like oaks of righteousness next to streams of water; if they don't, they will shrivel from drought and famine. As in Deuteronomy, the way of the kingdom is presented as a choice between life and death.

To have life they are to fear the Lord, acquire wisdom, follow the Torah, and trust that suffering is the way in which God grows his people. They should not accuse God of abandoning them in the midst of suffering, but rather use such times to search their hearts for sin and take comfort in the shadow of the Almighty. The Wisdom Literature is integral to a holistic picture of the kingdom. It instructs the people what life in the land of the kingdom is to look like. But like the rest of the Old Testament, it also reminds them that they do not yet have the king they have been waiting for.

The Story Continues: Warring Kingdoms

The Hebrew Scriptures conclude by returning to the narrative and giving perspective from the exile. Exile was a tangible form of judgment because it dislodged Israel from their land. Two snapshots of life out of place are provided in Esther and Daniel, then kingdom hope again revives for the people as they return to their place in Ezra and Nehemiah. The Hebrew Scriptures close with Chronicles, a final reflection on the history of God's people from Adam to that present day. Despite the exile, God is still establishing his kingdom through—even in spite of—the people.

Living Out of Place

Exiled because of their sin, the people suffer under a foreign king in a foreign land. But Yahweh has not forgotten his people; he will arise and crush the kings who oppose him. In the meantime, the people of Israel are called to submit to foreign kings while maintaining loyalty to their true King and his covenant. In Esther and Daniel, the Lord raises up leaders to preserve his people in the midst of homelessness. The book of Esther tells the story of how Esther becomes the queen of Persian king Ahasuerus (486–464 BC). Through her courage, God preserves his people from annihilation in the midst of exile. A kingdom must have people to occupy it, so Yahweh preserves his people through the bravery of Esther. Esther illustrates the war between the kingdom of men and the kingdom of God and survival by the most unexpected means.

Daniel also addresses Israel in exile (605–536 BC) but presents a unique, apocalyptic focus on God's authority over every kingdom. The curtain is pulled back multiple times in Daniel, revealing the rise and fall of human kingdoms. Each time, however, the kingdom of God outlasts them all. Though the people are in exile, God's kingdom will conquer. Meanwhile, the people still need to obey the King's covenantal law in a foreign land. Daniel becomes a prime example.

He rises to prominence not because he acquiesces to earthly kingdoms but because he is faithful to the Torah. Shadrach, Meshach, and Abednego are saved not because they compromise but because they stand firm. Alternately, the book of Daniel shows that those who do not humble themselves before the King of kings will be chastened. When King Nebuchadnezzar boasts in his own glory, he is stripped of his kingdom and becomes insane for seven years.

Nebuchadnezzar's son King Belshazzar acts in brash arrogance, taking the vessels that had been captured from the Jerusalem temple and drinking from them (Dan. 5:3–4). Daniel tells him he has lifted himself up against the Lord of heaven (Dan. 5:22). Belshazzar's kingdom falls that very night.

Three images are used in the book to represent the great kingdoms in Daniel: statues, trees, and beasts. In Daniel 2 the image of a statue is employed. The different metals on the various parts of the statue represent the strength of different kingdoms (vv. 31–33). But a stone rolls down and strikes the image and grows into a great mountain that fills the whole earth (vv. 34–35). Daniel interprets this dream as a vision of kingdoms. Nebuchadnezzar's kingdom is strong, but each one after his will be weaker. The stone that rolls down is from the God of heaven who will set up a kingdom that shall never be destroyed. The vision Daniel receives, along with the rest of Israel in exile, is that God will destroy the kingdom of man. Israel will not be left in exile forever.

In Daniel 4 the kingdom is portrayed by a tree. Nebuchadnezzar dreams of a magnificent tree that holds sway over the earth (vv. 10–12). But someone chops the tree down, lopping off its branches and scattering the birds and beasts taking shelter beneath (v. 14). Daniel reveals that this tree is Nebuchadnezzar and his kingdom. His kingdom will be chopped down until he learns that the Most High rules the kingdom of men (v. 25). Like the statue, the tree displays the power of God's kingdom over the kingdoms of mankind. It also shows once again that the kingdom is concerned with the king, his people, and their place. The birds and the beasts find comfort under the tree, which symbolizes people flourishing under good leadership. The people of Israel living in exile wonder if God is still King over all. Yahweh promises them through these dreams that his hand controls and directs all other kingdoms.

The third apocalyptic vision depicts the warring of kingdoms. Four kingdoms are described as four beasts (Dan. 7:1–8). These kingdoms devastate everything in their path. Their way of life is beastly, a foil to everything in the Wisdom Literature about the good life. Their reign will not endure forever, for the Ancient of Days sits upon his throne. Suddenly, "one like a son of man" comes to the Ancient of Days, and the kingdom is given to him. "All peoples, nations, and languages should serve him; his dominion is an everlasting dominion, which shall not pass away, and his kingdom one that shall not be destroyed" (Dan. 7:9–14). Here we can see the power of this son of man. The beasts are destroyed by this new kingdom (Dan. 7:26), and the kingdom is given to the saints: "But the saints of the Most High shall receive the kingdom and possess the kingdom forever, forever and ever" (Dan. 7:18).

All these visions concern the victory of the kingdom of heaven. Through this mysterious "son of man," the Ancient of Days accomplishes his purpose. The kingdom is handed over to the saints of the Most High. Both Esther and Daniel have pulled back the curtain of history to show that in the midst of exile, Yahweh is still preserving his people. His kingdom will be victorious in due time. Though the people of God are not in their land, they look forward to a time when Yahweh will conquer their enemies and reinstate his rightful rule over all creation. In that day, they will rule with him and bring blessings to all nations.

Rebuilding Their Kingdom

The people of Israel have seen the horizon, but the dawn of hope is slow and gradual. Ezra and Nehemiah recount how the people are allowed to return and rebuild Jerusalem. Glimmers of light shine through the dark window as the foreign rulers allow the people to return to their land and reconstruct their city. Will their true King be revealed at this time? Will they now dwell safely in their home?

The book of Ezra begins with a decree of Cyrus, the king of Persia, declaring that Israel can return and build a temple in Jerusalem (Ezra 1:1–3). The global picture of warring kingdoms in Esther and Daniel is repeated here as rebuilding of the temple walls is met with opposition. Yet the people, through the help of the prophets, endure through opposition and continue rebuilding.

Nehemiah gives a similar picture, focusing on restoring the walls of the city. For Jews, these two places (the city and the temple) were at the center of their devotion to Yahweh and their kingdom hope. The prophets had foretold that one day, all nations would stream into Jerusalem and worship Yahweh. A kingdom without Jerusalem or the temple was inconceivable. After the walls are built, Nehemiah makes plans to repopulate Jerusalem (chaps. 7; 11). The people of Israel finally return to their place, and kingdom life can commence. Yet the exile continues even though Israel is in their land, because they still live under the vassalage of other powers. They are still in exile because they have not obeyed the covenant. Nehemiah summarizes the message in a few verses:

> We [the people] have acted very corruptly against you and have not kept the commandments, the statutes, and the rules that you commanded your servant Moses. Remember the word that you commanded your servant Moses, saying, "If you are unfaithful, I will scatter you among the peoples, but if you return to me and keep my commandments and do them, though your outcasts are in the uttermost parts of heaven, from there I will gather them and bring them to the place that I have chosen, to make my name dwell there." (Neh. 1:7–9)

Unfortunately, the people find that they still can't keep the covenant. They are still awaiting the mysterious "son of man" figure to bring them out of exile. Although they are back in their land, things are still not as they should be.

Where Is the Kingdom? A Final Commentary

The canon of the Hebrew Scriptures closes with a prophetic and theological commentary on the history of Israel. As Genesis begins with Adam, so Chronicles opens its narrative with Adam. Both books trace the progress of the seed through genealogies (people). The Chronicler writes at the time when the people of Israel are being restored from their captivity in Babylon, when there is uncertainty. The Chronicler attempts to answer the questions of God's people: Who are we? How did we get here? What happened? And what must we do?

Despite the exile, the author is making the case that God is still in charge, and he will bring restoration. The placement of this book as the last one in the Hebrew Scriptures provides a theological homily on all of Israel's history. As Scott Hahn says:

> [He] aims to do far more than retell Israel's national story. He is delivering a word of divine assurance. He wants his readers to understand the history he is retelling is not finished: it is ongoing. . . . The Chronicler's intent is to remind Judah's people of God's original intentions—not only for Israel, but also for creation—and to help align their hearts and lives more faithfully with that divine plan. A prophetic exhortation attributed to King Jehoshaphat could serve as a summary of his authorial purposes in the book. "Hear me, Judah and inhabitants of Jerusalem! Believe the Lord your God, and you will be established; believe his prophets and you will succeed" (2 Chron. 20:20).[7]

---

7. Scott Hahn, *The Kingdom of God as Liturgical Empire: A Theological Commentary on 1–2 Chronicles* (Grand Rapids, MI: Baker Academic, 2012), 3.

The Chronicler believes that God's covenant establishes his kingship. Through the chronological outline, the author traces the story from Adam, through Noah, to Abraham, to Israel, and finally to David with whom God makes an everlasting covenant (2 Chron. 13:5; 21:7).

This outline helps Israel see that through covenant Yahweh is advancing his kingdom. The goal is to fulfill the threefold promise made to Abraham: to make him into a great nation, to give him a great name, and to make him a source of blessing for all nations. The people of Israel are all members of the same family, and they share a common covenant, ancestry, and story.[8] The Chronicler is convinced that this family has a *telos* (end goal), which can be summarized in the word *kingdom*.

Just as Genesis ends with the people in exile, so Chronicles ends with the people in exile. But together they cling to the promise of return from exile. In Genesis 50:24 Joseph remarks, "I am about to die, but God will visit you and *bring you up out* of this land [Egypt] that he swore to Abraham, to Isaac, and to Jacob." Chronicles ends in a similar way, as Cyrus the King of Persia declares, "The LORD, the God of heaven, has given me all the kingdoms of the earth, and he has charged me to build him a house at Jerusalem, which is in Judah. Whoever is among you of all his people, may the LORD his God be with him. *Let him go up*" (2 Chron. 36:23).

God is going to establish his kingdom, and someone will lead them up out of exile. He has not forgotten his promises to Abraham and David. The whole world will be able to see the tree of Israel someday. God's purposes for this nation must be fulfilled through the enigmatic Son of Man, the servant, the son of David, the Messiah.

---

8. Ibid., 9.

The Kingdom in the Writings

The Writings are not extraneous to the story of the kingdom. The poetic sections paint a picture of what it means to flourish (or be blessed) under the rule of the king. Many of these writings come from the kings of Israel who were to embody the law for the people and lead them in following the covenant. Israel was to fear the Lord and obey the Torah, understanding that suffering is part of the kingdom plan, not antithetical to it. But even in the Wisdom Literature it is evident they are still waiting for their King.

As the poetic section comes to an end, the narrative picks up again, this time showing what life east of Eden looks like. Daniel has visions that display the kingdom of God vanquishing the kingdom of man. Ezra and Nehemiah are sent back to rebuild their city and the temple, and the Chronicler closes out the Hebrew Scriptures by giving a prophetic and theological history of the people of Israel. God is still working out his promises despite the sin of the people.

The kingdom is still coming. There will be someone who ends the exile, washes the people clean, remakes them, restores their fortunes, and establishes the mountain of the Lord as the highest mountain.

Summary: The Kingdom in the Hebrew Scriptures

The Hebrew Scriptures begin with God enthroned as Sabbath King. He created all things by his words, and he constructed a kingdom tree in the garden that would grow straight and true. But there is another tree in the garden, and Adam and Eve face a choice—will they choose from the tree of life or the tree of death? They choose to listen to the Serpent, eating from the tree of death, and therefore their children toil under the pressure to build their own kingdom.

Chaos, destruction, and heartache are the result. Yet, despite their faithlessness, and running parallel to this dark portrait, sprout the promises of God. Although the people's efforts strip the tree bare, God pledges to grow his kingdom through the covenants he makes with Abraham, Moses, and David. The kingdom will come through covenant. Kingdom hope thus *revives* with the story of Abraham, and the good kingdom is *foreshadowed* in the Prophets. The Writings give a glimpse at *life in the kingdom* under the good King.

But to live, the people must first go through the death process of winter. Though the aroma of kingdom hope is still present, God gives them over to their sin to reveal that he must accomplish his mission. The climactic result is the exile. The tree has been chopped down to the stump. But God has already planted the kingdom seed in the ground (Gen. 3:15). One of Abraham's children, from the line of Judah, the seed of David, will grow up out of the stump and will lead them to the place beside still waters. God's plan is to make a *place*, through a future *King*, so that his *people* might dwell with him again.

The Hebrew Scriptures thus mingle the darkness of human sin with the light of the hope of a coming kingdom. This bright kingdom is portrayed not with lifeless colors but with the vibrant realness of life. The kingdom that Israel seeks has walls, wells, and gates. Inside the city there will be food, markets, and families. Most importantly, a throne will be at the center of the city. But as the curtain closes on the Old Testament, Israel still does not know who will sit on that throne.

PART 2

KINGDOM IN THE
NEW TESTAMENT

4

The Gospels

Embodying the Kingdom

We expect the King to come into the world with a bang. To conquer, destroy, win, and set up his kingdom. But he comes quietly—in a little town in the corner of the world. Rather than conquering, he is conquered. Rather than overthrowing, he is trod into the very dirt. He is broken, with bowed head and lowered eyes, shoulders falling down like teardrops—but still, he rises.[1] Maya Angelou, a famous African American poet and a confidant of Martin Luther King Jr., writes:

> You may tread me in the very dirt
> But still, like dust, I'll rise.[2]

Jesus is killed with hate and also trod in the very dirt. Yet it is only

---

1 See Maya Angelou, "Still I Rise," in *The Complete Collected Poems of Maya Angelou* (New York: Random House, 1994), 163.

2. Ibid.

through being conquered that he installs the kingdom that was promised long ago.

Gospels and Kingdom

As the scenes in the Gospels unfold, expectations grow as the new King is slowly revealed. The promises made to Adam, Abraham, David, and Isaiah are brought to fulfillment through this Davidic Messiah. But shock and dismay also fill the moment, for the King that was prophesied to lead them into the kingdom dies. He is killed with hate—but still, he rises.

Jesus shows them that the kingdom will not be realized by means of a large army. The means will be more like a seed planted in the ground (Matt. 13:24–32). It is like leaven placed in bread rather than the sudden appearance of high walls and a throne. The kingdom is compared to a mustard seed, or a net thrown into the sea, or a merchant in search of fine pearls. In one sense the good news of the kingdom *is* what the Jews were expecting: it fulfilled the promises that their enemies would be vanquished, the temple would be rebuilt, and they would occupy their land.

However, all these things did not happen *when* or *how* they expected. They expected a kingdom achieved with a warrior on a white horse. What they saw was a man from Nazareth who had no place to lay his head. He rode into Jerusalem not on a stallion but on a donkey. Moreover, in Jerusalem, he did not sit on his throne but marched to Golgotha with a tree on his back. Thus, the kingdom is both like and unlike the Jews' expectations.

A similarity and a dissimilarity exist between the Gospel presentations and what the Jews were anticipating. Jesus's revelations about the kingdom are sufficient to get him murdered by worldly powers but sufficiently veiled to confuse his disciples (Acts 1:6). As one scholar notes, "the new element in the preaching of John and Jesus, then, was not that they spoke of the Kingdom of Heaven, but that they proclaimed its being at hand."[3] Everything Jesus says or does in some way relates to the kingdom and how it is at hand. How can this be so?

It can be so because Jesus is *the kingdom.*[4] Jesus alone truly fulfills the demands of the kingdom. He personalizes it, embodies it, and takes his seat on the throne. What Adam, Abraham, Joseph, Moses, Joshua, Samson, Saul, David, and Daniel disrupted, Jesus mollified. Jesus is the human face of the kingdom.

The Fourfold Witness

So how does one tackle the kingdom in the four Gospels? The centrality of the Gospels for the interpretation of the kingdom is difficult to overstate. One method is to look at the fourfold witness in harmony, focusing on themes. This is a well-worn road in biblical theology. But we did not receive a jumbo gospel; we received a fourfold gospel. The early church under the Spirit's guidance perceived that one gospel could not accomplish all that needed to be said about Jesus, so they gave us a kaleidoscopic view of his life. To reduce this fourfold witness to a unified vision obscures just as many things as it clarifies. Therefore, we will examine the distinctive aspects of the kingdom that each Gospel writer brings into focus.

We will see that Matthew focuses on the place of the kingdom, using the unique phrase "the kingdom of heaven." Jesus comes as the King in Matthew, the seed of David, who reorders the place of the earth to make it look more like heaven. Mark emphasizes the King's authority. In fact, Mark uses the word *authority* in a higher concentration than any other Gospel writer.[5] Luke directs his gaze to those who will inherit the kingdom. The weak, the poor, the neglected, and

---

3. Herman N. Ridderbos, *When the Time Had Fully Come: Studies in New Testament Theology* (Grand Rapids, MI: Eerdmans, 1957), 14.

4. As Origen said, Jesus is the αὐτόβασιλεία.

5. Both Matthew and Mark use ἐξουσία ten times. Luke uses it sixteen times, but Mark still uses it more in terms of percentage of words.

the unexpected will enter the kingdom. Finally, we will discover that John presents the kingdom similar to the Wisdom Literature, through the lens of life, or even eternal life.[6] In each Gospel, Jesus reframes, confirms, and even adjusts the disciples' view of the kingdom.

Matthew	The King's place
Mark	The King's power
Luke	The King's people
John	Life in the kingdom

Matthew: The King's Place

In Matthew, Jesus establishes the kingdom as a radical alternative to all the earthly foils of the kingdom. He arrives as the King, the seed of David, who accomplishes Adam's task of ordering the place of the earth to make it look like heaven. The first Gospel speaks of "the kingdom of heaven" rather than "the kingdom of God." This unique phrase should be interpreted in light of the tension between heaven and earth that began in Genesis 3. Matthew contrasts heaven and earth consistently in his Gospel, drawing a sharp distinction between these realms. There is the heavenly kingdom and the earthly kingdom. Jesus unites these realms in his ministry through the incarnation. The presence of the King is key to the book of Matthew.

Matthew begins by rendering Jesus's story as the continuation of Israel's story. Jesus retraces the footsteps of Israel while correcting their missteps, thereby bringing blessings to the whole world. But he does so in a strange way. Rather than ruling immediately, he is chased by another king. Rather than conquering with the sword, he heals. Rather than rebuilding the temple, he says it will be destroyed.

---

6. As I argue these emphases in each Gospel, I acknowledge the divisions are not entirely neat. Matthew also focuses on Jesus's authority as a teacher. Mark speaks of Isaiah's new exodus, part and parcel of the kingdom announcement. Luke by no means neglects the place of the kingdom. Yet in these multifaceted works, I want to underline a theme particular to each Gospel.

In some of Jesus's first words, in the Sermon on the Mount, he again presents an upside-down kingdom; he blesses the poor in spirit and the persecuted. Jesus contrasts a heavenly ethic to the earthly code that had been governing since the time of Adam. Jesus's Torah comes in the form of distinct heaven-earth contrasts: "Do not lay up for yourselves treasures *on earth*, where moth and rust destroy and where thieves break in and steal, but lay up for yourselves treasures *in heaven*" (Matt. 6:19–20). Jesus juxtaposes the values of the kingdoms of earth with those of the kingdom of heaven. He brings a new cadence to the rhythms of this world.

Jesus continues to connect heaven and earth through his words in the kingdom parables (Matthew 13). Jesus builds his kingdom not through a sword but through a message. His words, like seeds, go into the earth and sprout the kingdom through people, transforming place. The parables show that the kingdom is not as the Jews expected in terms of timing, nature, or means. The Jews thought that the tree would be fully mature when the kingdom arrived, but Jesus shows that the tree must grow and expand in and through people. Also, his people (the church) mysteriously unite the realms of heaven and earth (Matt. 16:19; 18:18). This is possible only because Jesus promises that he, the King of heaven, will be present with the church. Jesus's presence changes the space of the earth and the nature of his community.

Jesus also brings place into being through his deeds of healing, exorcism, and forgiveness. The land is made a foretaste of heaven as he goes about touching people with compassion and authority. In the Beelzebul controversy (Matthew 12), Jesus contests Satan, the lord of the earth, and plunders his property, thereby crushing the kingdom of earth with the kingdom of heaven. Rather than conquering Rome, Jesus conquers the true enemy. By the Spirit, Jesus rewrites the space of the earth. The turning point of the narrative occurs when Jesus heads to Jerusalem for the first time (Matt. 16:21). Jesus, as the Son of David, intends to return to the city of the King. Jesus was exiled from his home, but he returns from exile and brings his people with him.

After Jesus enters Jerusalem riding a donkey, he warns the people about rejecting their King, predicts the destruction of the temple, and allows his body to be suspended at the center of the cosmos on a tree. The rulers of this earth crucify him as a false king, and his disciples abandon him. As he is crucified, the earth trembles and bodies rise from the grave. Ultimately the place of the earth cannot hold him fast. A hole tears in the earth, the temple curtain is torn, and the Father vindicates the life of the Son by way of resurrection.

He comes to find himself in a garden, the place where it all started in Genesis. The kingdom of heaven has come through the incarnation, death, and resurrection of the King.

> The resurrection of Jesus . . . is the reaffirmation of the universe of space, time and matter. . . . The early Christians saw Jesus's resurrection as the action of the creator god to reaffirm the essential goodness of creation and, in an initial and representative act of new creation, to establish a bridgehead within the present world of space, time and matter . . . through which the whole new creation could now come to birth.[7]

The resurrected Jesus meets his disciples on a mountain, a place linking heaven and earth. He sends them out to proclaim his authority. By his presence, Jesus contests the kingdoms of the earth, installing the kingdom of heaven on earth. Matthew forges a bond between heaven and earth through the presence of Jesus. "The presence of

---

7. N. T. Wright, *The Resurrection of the Son of God*, vol. 3, Christian Origins and the Question of God (Minneapolis: Fortress Press, 2003), 729–30.

Jesus becomes heaven's link with the earthly gathering."[8] Indeed, all authority in heaven and earth is now his. Matthew gives a picture of the presence of the heavenly King conquering earthly space through his words and deeds. He embodied the kingdom upon the earth, but it was a kingdom they did not expect.

Mark: The King's Power

While one of Matthew's main concentrations is the place of the kingdom, Mark employs different titles and descriptions for Jesus to indicate the authority of the King. If Matthew looks at the place of the kingdom, Mark looks at the power of the King, radically redefining it through service and suffering. The opening line of Mark's Gospel functions as a title for the book: "The beginning of the gospel of Jesus Christ, the Son of God" (Mark 1:1).

Just as Adam was made in the image of God to rule and shape the earth, so too Jesus is the Son of God completing this task. Later a voice from heaven twice acknowledges Jesus's authority as the Son of God (Mark 1:11; 9:7). Then when Jesus crosses paths with unclean spirits, they too recognize him as the Son of God (Mark 3:11; 5:7). Mark carries this theme throughout the book until the climax of the narrative when the centurion declares Jesus is the Son of God at the cross (Mark 15:39). The title "Son of God" echoes from the halls of royalty. In 2 Samuel 7 and Psalm 2 the term is tied to kingship. He rules as King, the anointed Messiah, acting on behalf of and in union with God's will. Thus, Mark's first words identify Jesus as the King who acts for the Father upon the earth. Yet clarity comes for readers only when they see the centurion confessing Jesus as the Son of God on the cross. The power of the King is manifested in suffering.

---

8. David Kupp, *Matthew's Emmanuel: Divine Presence and God's People in the First Gospel* (Cambridge, UK: Cambridge University Press, 1996), 182.

Mark also speaks of the good news similarly to Matthew: "The time is fulfilled, and the kingdom of God is at hand; repent and believe in the gospel" (Mark 1:15). Mark points the spotlight on Jesus himself; the kingdom arrives in the person and power of Jesus. In Mark, there is a strong emphasis on the time aspect of the kingdom. Jesus now has power over demons, disease, death, and nature. He casts out impure spirits in the synagogue. Mark specifically notes that the people are astonished at his teaching, for he teaches them as one who has authority (Mark 1:22). An exorcism demonstrates this authority, and the crowds marvel once more (Mark 1:27).

Jesus continues his authoritative ministry by performing various healings. He even claims that the "Son of Man has authority on the earth to forgive sins" (Mark 2:10). "Son of Man" is Jesus's preferred title, taken from Daniel 7:13–14. There, the son of man rides the clouds and receives authority from God. It's a title ambiguous enough for Jesus to use, but it also functions as a representative idea for humanity.

Jesus fulfills Adam's role of ruling the kingdom for God as the true human. The term takes on further authority when understood in Daniel's context. The beasts of Daniel stand in contrast to the image of the son of man who received authority. However, just as the Son of God's meaning is revealed at the cross, the authority of the Son of Man is revealed at the resurrection as he is enthroned and receives authority from God.

The authority of Jesus meets various kinds of opposition. Jesus's own family goes out to seize him because he is out of his mind. The teachers of the law claim that Beelzebul possesses Jesus. Interestingly, in the Beelzebul episode the teachers of the law recognize his power—the debate is about the *source* of his authority (Mark 3:22).

Jesus continues demonstrating his authority as the King of the universe by exercising power over nature (Mark 4:35–41), over demons (Mark 5:1–20), and over sickness (Mark 5:21–43). Again the paradox arises that people do not submit to Jesus's authority. People of his hometown ask, "Where did this man get these things? What is the wisdom given to him?" (Mark 6:2). Jesus is rejected in his hometown. Over and over again, Jesus's kingly power is made clear, but various groups question, deny, or reject the new King.

So Jesus turns his face toward Jerusalem (Mark 8:22). On the way to Jerusalem, Jesus is transfigured before them (Mark 9:2–8) and declared to be the Son of God. Jesus shows this select group that he is the King they have been waiting for. Mark puts the titles "Messiah" and "Son of God" in close proximity in the transfiguration just as he did at the opening of his book (Mark 1:1). These two titles interpret each other. Jesus is revealing who he is and what he must do, but the disciples are slow to understand.

In Jerusalem, three episodes help frame the power and authority of the King: Jesus's actions in the temple, Jesus on the cross, and Jesus in his resurrection. Jesus enters Jerusalem, and people say that David's kingdom is coming (Mark 11:10). Yet when he enters the temple, he does not restore it; rather, he pronounces its destruction. The power of the King was supposed to vanquish the Jews' enemies, but Jesus condemns the Jewish authorities for their actions. The Pharisees try to trick him, the Sadducees question him, and a scribe tests him. No one recognizes the authority of the Son of God; they seek to entrap him. This is similar to the previous sections, but the narrative in Jerusalem has heightened the drama. In a climactic section of Mark, Jesus declares that he is David's Son and David's Lord, possessing all authority (Mark 12:35–37).

Even as Jesus is betrayed to his death, the narrative indicates that Jesus is in full control of the situation. First, the woman at Bethany anoints Jesus for his burial (Mark 14:3–9). Second, Jesus speaks of the one among the disciples who will betray him (Mark 14:17–21). Third,

Jesus foretells Peter's denial (Mark 14:26–31). Fourth, Jesus acknowledges the Father's will and allows himself to be arrested (Mark 14:42, 49). Fifth, Jesus remains silent before the councils (Mark 14:61). Finally, Jesus accepts his death before the mockers, and the centurion declares him to be the Son of God (Mark 15:39). The Son of God not only accepts his fate but controls it as the King of the kingdom. He knows that the way to the kingdom is by giving his life as a ransom for many (Mark 10:45). In Jesus's death, he exhibits his power over Satan.

Mark closes with the resurrection of Jesus, which points to Jesus's enthronement as the King of the kingdom. Jesus parades his authority over death and creation in the resurrection. The women are afraid when they see the angel (Mark 16:5). They are also afraid when they leave. Then suddenly the narrative stops. The authority of the King has been established through the most shocking means: a bloody cross and an empty tomb. The resurrection broadcasts the power of the King. Mark leaves his readers with the question, Now what will you do?

Luke: The King's People

If Matthew shows Jesus transforming the place of the kingdom, and Mark emphasizes the power of the King, then Luke focuses on the people who will occupy the kingdom. Luke emphasizes how Jesus helps the marginal, the rejected, the poor, tax collectors, sinners, women, Samaritans, and Gentiles. The socially, politically, and spiritually disadvantaged individuals are welcomed. Many of Luke's accounts would have chaffed his readers as he criticizes both the rich and the supposed "faithful" while anticipating the kingdom. Just as Matthew presents the upside-down kingdom, and Mark the authority of the King through suffering, now Luke shows that the people of the King are those on the fringe. Christ did not die for the good and beautiful.

Luke's Gospel opens with the good news of a ruler to whom poor shepherds pay homage. The Gospel closes with a ruler who spurns the King, revealing that the kingdom is a dent in the norms of civil and political society. The genealogy in Luke rewinds all the way back to Adam, indicating that Jesus is the Savior of all mankind (Luke 3:38) who came to bring *shalom* to all people.

A crucial passage for Luke's portrayal of Jesus's ministry comes when he stands up in the synagogue to read from Isaiah. Here he speaks of the Spirit of the Lord anointing him to proclaim good news to the poor, proclaim liberty to the captives, and recover the sight of the blind (Luke 4:18–19). This anointing indicates that the King is coming for those in captivity. Luke designates Jesus's ministry as one where the King descends from heaven to welcome the captives. In the Sermon on the Plain, Jesus blesses the poor, the hungry, and the weeping. He pronounces woes upon those who are rich, full, and laughing (Luke 5:20–26).

Luke's account of Jesus's actions indicates that he comes for the marginalized. He heals the servant of a centurion—a representative of Roman oppression and everything the Jews were trying to overcome. Then he raises a widow's son. Widows had no social standing. Luke goes out of his way to highlight the women who accompany Jesus (Luke 8:1–3). The twelve apostles are to act like Jesus, taking nothing with them (Luke 9:1–6), denying themselves, and taking up their cross and following Jesus (Luke 9:23–27). Those who will enter the kingdom must love their neighbor in the manner of the Good Samaritan (Luke 10:25–37).

Jesus's journey to Jerusalem begins in Luke 9:51 as he tells more parables and performs various miracles illustrating that all are invited to the kingdom. The kingdom is for the lost sheep, the prodigal son, the faithful, and the poor. It is for the persistent widow, the Pharisee, the tax collector, and children. In one poignant episode,

Jesus welcomes the tax collector Zacchaeus, announcing that salvation has come to Zacchaeus's house (Luke 19:9).

In the context of Jesus's controversial actions, the Pharisees ask a temporal question: When will the kingdom of God come? (Luke 17:20–21). Jesus replies by telling them they do not understand the nature of the kingdom. The kingdom of God is coming in ways that cannot be observed: "The kingdom of God is in the midst of you" (v. 21). But they can't see it because they are blind. The King of the kingdom is standing right in front of them, and he is offering it to those they least expect.

The unexpected nature of the kingdom continues in the story of Jesus's death. Ultimately, he is convicted on the testimony of false witnesses and sent to the cross to die as a criminal. On the way to his execution, Jesus turns to those mourning for him and says, "Daughters of Jerusalem, do not weep for me, but weep for yourselves and for your children" (Luke 23:28).

Jerusalem and her leaders have rejected their King. They crucify Jesus on the tree, but death cannot swallow him; he rises again. He appears to his disciples and explains that all of this was according to plan. "Repentance for the forgiveness of sins should be proclaimed in his name *to all nations*, beginning from Jerusalem" (Luke 24:47). Jesus ascends after promising his people that the Spirit will come and help them in their mission.

Luke's picture of the people of the kingdom is culturally and ethically daring. More than that, it drives the religious leaders to plot his death. The kingdom in Luke is about the people of the King, and Jesus promises to give the kingdom to his disciples (Luke 12:32). The symbolic universe that Jesus is creating challenges the status quo and angers those around him. Yet Jesus knows this new world order will come about only when the King is sacrificed on the cross for the sins of all people, conquering the Devil, who rules their social milieu.

John: Life in the Kingdom

Compared to the Synoptics, John rarely uses the term *kingdom*. It is used twice in John 3 when Jesus is talking to Nicodemus (John 3:3, 5), and once at Jesus's trial when Jesus claims his kingdom is not of this world (John 18:36). The key term John uses to unfold the kingdom is *life* and its synonym *eternal life*. John even states that the purpose of his Gospel is that "you may believe that Jesus is the Christ, the Son of God, and that by believing you may have life in his name" (John 20:31). The concepts of life, Messiah, and belief are intertwined in this verse. If Messiah is connected to kingship, then *life* must be another metaphor for the kingdom. Life and the kingdom are mediated through Christ. If the Synoptics fulfill the narrative of the Hebrew Scriptures, then John's language maps to the Wisdom Literature.

So what is *life* for John? Just because *life* and *kingdom* are used interchangeably does not mean they are synonymous. Some suppose *life* is either a more personal way to speak of the kingdom or a spiritual way to designate it. But John presents life neither as an individualistic concept nor as merely spiritual. Jesus, the Word made flesh, is life. In John, Jesus gives life through material elements such as bread and water. The resurrection is said to be eternal life—not merely a spiritual resurrection but a bodily one. What then does John mean by *life* and *eternal life*?

Marianne Meye Thompson explains that the term *life* comes from the "understanding that God is the 'living God.' This means that life uniquely belongs to and characterizes God."[9] Life comes from God; the mediator of this life is Jesus Christ. Although one might be quick to relegate life to the future, *life* in John seems to be a reality lived fully in the present but also oriented toward the future. To "have life" in Christ is to have it now—and in the future. The kingdom is already

---

9. Marianne Meye Thompson, "Eternal Life in the Gospel of John," *Ex Auditu* 5 (1989): 45.

here because Jesus has inaugurated it, but it will be fully consummated in the future. The same is true in John of life and/or eternal life. So for John, *life* and *eternal life* are ways to clarify what it means to live in the kingdom.

Unlike the other Gospel writers, John uses images, most of them from the Hebrew Scriptures, to describe Jesus. Jesus is the light of the world who gives the light of life (John 8:12). He came to give eternal life; he is the resurrection and the life (John 11:25). His commandments are eternal life (John 12:50). Knowing Jesus is eternal life (John 17:3). John depicts the kingdom in terms that are not otherworldly but are experienced in the present.

However, the kingdom does have an otherworldly aspect, as Jesus claims at his trial. His kingdom will come not by coercion and dominance but through sacrifice. Eternal life is a view on reality that can already see the unseen divine realities at play. John's Gospel does not contradict the Synoptic presentation but complements that view of the kingdom by giving a comprehensive picture of the kingdom. Kingdom life is about salvation for God's people in their own place under the power of the King.

The Kingdom in the Gospels

The Hebrew Scriptures end with the people of God looking toward the horizon and straining to see when their deliverer will come. The Gospels announce his arrival. But it is both like and unlike what they expect. Each Gospel writer provides an account of Jesus's life and shows how he embodies the kingdom, fulfilling the Old Testament promises concerning power, people, and place.

Jesus is the seed of Abraham, the son of David, the new Moses. He is the son of man from Daniel, the servant from Isaiah, the shepherd from Zechariah. He is wisdom, Torah, and life. But he also is the one who reframes their view of the kingdom. He blesses those who mourn; he portrays the kingdom as a mustard seed that grows; he demonstrates his authority through agony; and he welcomes the unwelcome. So while he fulfills the hopes and dreams of Israel, he also clarifies and corrects their misconceptions.

The whole of Scripture culminates on a mountain, and at the top of it we find a tree—the cross. The Gospels present the kingdom realized through the cross. The cross establishes the kingdom; the kingdom comes through the cross. But if the kingdom is people and place, then the kingdom is also hidden beneath the people of God (the church). In Matthew, Jesus gives his people authority on the earth to enact kingdom influence (Matt. 16:19–20; 18:18–19). The cross lives on in the people of God and the places where they gather together. When they take up their crosses and follow Jesus, there the kingdom is.

There is a scene at the end of *The Lord of the Rings* where Aragorn stands at the edge of Mordor not knowing what has become of Sam and Frodo. He looks at the army in front of him and sees that they are too many for his meager troops. Tears come to his eyes as he thinks this is the end. But he raises his sword and charges nonetheless, running out before them all. Aragorn is willing to show his people what it means to sacrifice himself in the face of reckless evil so that they can live in their land in peace. In a similar way, Jesus is not only willing but actually sacrifices himself as the King of the kingdom. His death conquers death, and like Aragorn he is crowned as King so his people can rest in their new home.

When Abraham departed Ur, he left three things: his country (land), his kindred (people), and his father's house (power). God promised him he would gain three things in return: land, a great nation, and blessing. All three of these promises were fulfilled in Jesus. Jesus restored the land (Matthew), Jesus formed a new community (Luke), and Jesus was the promised ruler (Mark). A good summary statement of this truth is that those who submit to the King can have life (John), and the means that life comes to us is through the King's death.

The Gospels turn the page on the kingdom story. Jesus moves the kingdom story from one of promise to one of fulfillment, from hope to satisfaction, from potential to reality. The kingdom Adam failed to obtain is now here in Jesus's ministry. The Gospels not only bring the story of Israel to a climax but continue it. For while the kingdom is at hand in the person of Jesus, it also will not be consummated until the very end.

5

Acts and the Epistles

Kingdom Community

At the end of his Gospel, John mentions that the sign placed over Jesus on the cross was written in three languages: Aramaic, Latin, and Greek (John 19:20). The sign read, "Jesus of Nazareth, the King of the Jews." John's irony is thick. The Romans inscribed this sign as a declaration for why this man was crucified, but in the providence of God, it announced to the whole known world that the true King had arrived. Now that the death and resurrection of the King have taken place, it is time to declare and form the community of the King from every tongue, tribe, and nation. If the Gospels introduce readers to the King, then the rest of the New Testament traces the expansion, advance, and hope of the King's community.

Enter the book of Acts. The purpose of Acts is to give assurance that the events of the early church advance the kingdom story; despite the weakness and suffering of God's people, God is still fulfilling his kingdom plan through Jesus and his people. Luke, the author, is writing not only history but biblical history, a sacred narrative, a continuation of the story of the seed first announced in Genesis 3. Acts is positioned between the Gospels and the Epistles and shows the spread of the kingdom. The kingdom was embodied in Jesus but not in the way they expected. Now it will continue to grow but, again, not in the way they expect. Suffering marks the road ahead.

Law	Reviving hope in the kingdom
Prophets	Foreshadowing the kingdom
Writings	Life in the kingdom
Gospels	Embodying the kingdom
Acts and Epistles	**Kingdom community**

Acts

If Acts stands as the bridge between the Gospels and the Epistles, then it would be natural to assume that the prevalence of the kingdom language that begins in the Gospels would continue in the rest of the New Testament. But a quick word search shows this is not the case. Kingdom language is relegated to only a few instances from here on out.

This does not mean the concept of the kingdom is inconsequential. The kingdom stands at the forefront of the minds of the apostles. Similar to other biblical narratives, Acts shows that the risen Lord's *power* is given to *people* through the Holy Spirit, and they spread this message to every *place* ("the end of the earth," Acts 1:8). The tree that was in the garden is spreading through the sacrifice of the King and the suffering of his people.

Kingdom Framing

Acts falls within the framework of God's kingdom. This must be so, since Luke's Gospel centers on the arrival of the kingdom in Christ, and Acts is in a sense part 2 to Luke's Gospel. It would be incongruous in a self-proclaimed sequel volume (Acts 1:1–2) if the author were to abandon a central theme. Almost immediately in the narrative of Acts we see that the idea of *kingdom* is on Luke's mind.

The term first appears in Acts 1:3 as Jesus teaches his disciples for forty days about the kingdom of God before he returns to the Father. A few verses later the disciples gather around him and ask, "Will you at this time restore the kingdom to Israel?" (Acts 1:6). These two references to the kingdom at the beginning of the book set up the rest of the narrative.

Another reference to the kingdom comes at the conclusion of Acts. In Acts 28:23, 31, Paul is imprisoned in Rome, but the Word of the Lord is still going forth. The local Jewish leaders arrange to meet Paul, and "from morning till evening he expounded to them, testifying to the kingdom of God" (v. 23). Acts finishes with the picture of Paul proclaiming the kingdom of God with all boldness and without hindrance (v. 31). As Thompson says, in both of "these contexts there is an emphasis on the comprehensive teaching about the kingdom of God."[1] In Acts 1:3 it is Jesus's teaching, and in Acts 20:31 Luke closes his narrative with a summary statement of Paul's preaching. The summary of Jesus's message and the summary of Paul's message in Acts center on one term: *kingdom*.

When the disciples ask about the restoration of the kingdom in Acts 1:7–8, Jesus responds in two ways. First, in verse 7, Jesus says, "It is not for you to know times or seasons that the Father has fixed by his own authority." He rejects their attempt to calculate the timing. However, he goes on to say in verse 8, "But you will receive power when the Holy Spirit has come upon you, and you will be my witnesses in Jerusalem and in all Judea and Samaria, and to the end of the earth."

---

1. Alan Thompson, *The Acts of the Risen Lord Jesus: Luke's Account of God's Unfolding Plan*, New Studies in Biblical Theology (Downers Grove, IL: InterVarsity Press, 2011), 44.

Luke validates a close connection between the Holy Spirit and the kingdom. The Holy Spirit is the answer to the kingdom question.

The language of restoration also recalls the hopes of God's gift of the Spirit for his people. Therefore, when the disciples ask if Jesus is going to restore the kingdom to Israel, he reframes how they are to think of it in terms of receiving the Holy Spirit and being witnesses to all the known world of his kingship. In the very next verses the disciples witness Jesus's ascension to his heavenly throne. The kingdom will now advance by the authority of the exalted King, by the power of the Spirit, and through his people in the proclamation of the gospel.

Geography in Acts

The spread, or the geographical movement, of the kingdom is maybe the most fundamental point of Acts. Acts 1:8 gives a summary of the book: "But you will receive power when the Holy Spirit has come upon you, and you will be my witnesses in Jerusalem and in all Judea and Samaria, and to the end of the earth." The power of the Holy Spirit drives the witnesses and their kingdom message to every corner of the earth.

Acts traces the spread of the gospel of the kingdom from Jerusalem all the way to Rome. This is not only a geographical outline; it is a theo-political statement. Israel must be symbolically reconstituted with Jerusalem at its center. Then the northern and the southern kingdoms—Judea and Samaria—must be reconciled. Finally, and only after these events, the gospel goes to the Gentiles. Visually, Acts looks like this:

Jerusalem → Judea → Samaria → Ends of the Earth (Rome)

The direction of the biblical story is from the particular to the universal. Geographically, the narrative begins by focusing on one place (Jerusalem), but it is to flow from one place to every place. Just like in the Hebrew Scriptures, the blessings pass in and through Israel and their kings. But unlike the Hebrew Scriptures, everything is going out of Jerusalem rather than coming in. Scott Hahn rightfully states:

> Jesus' geographical description of the spread of the gospel ... is a *Davidic map* that reflects the *theological geography* of God's covenant pledge concerning the extent of the Davidic empire.... The kingdom of David ... will be restored as the apostles' witness extends to "the ends of the earth" and the ἐκκλησία [church] grows.[2]

The sermons that appear throughout the book of Acts carry the kingdom message into these successive geographical regions and recount three things.[3] First, each sermon focuses on the life, death, and resurrection of Jesus. There seems to be a special focus on the resurrection as the vindication of Jesus's identity as *the King* (continuing the theme of the Gospels). Second, the sermons connect the life of Jesus and the coming of the Holy Spirit as the inauguration of the kingdom. Finally, each sermon indicates that this narrative about Jesus fulfills the Scriptures.

Kingdom Themes in the Sermons of Acts	
Resurrection	Christ is King
Holy Spirit	Inauguration of the kingdom
Plan of God	Fulfillment of the Scriptures

Even a cursory look at the sermons in Acts indicates that the kingship of Christ is still their message.

---

2. Scott Hahn, "Kingdom and Church in Luke–Acts: From Davidic Christology to Kingdom Ecclesiology," in *Reading Luke: Interpretation, Reflections, Formation*, Scripture and Hermeneutics 6 (Grand Rapids, MI: Zondervan, 2005), 316.

3. Although there is some variation, due to the context of each crowd. Yet the three points I raise above seem to be a pattern of preaching.

So Luke, through the sermons in Acts, teaches us about the importance of the resurrection for the kingdom story, because Christ is declared as King through both the cross and the resurrection. He also tells of the relationship of the Holy Spirit to the kingdom story; the Holy Spirit is sent to empower the community to continue this kingdom mission. All of this is put into the framework of kingdom communities spreading as local congregations throughout the whole known world. Paul establishes churches in key cities and appoints elders to carry on his work. Although the King has returned to the Father, the people of the kingdom are spreading to every place through the power of the Holy Spirit and the preaching of the Word.

The Exalted and Risen King

Luke not only frames his narrative in Acts with kingdom references, ties the kingdom to the pouring out of the Holy Spirit, and includes sermons centered on the vindication of Christ through resurrection from the dead, but he also centers on the acts of the exalted and risen Lord. Acts is not only the acts of the apostles and the acts of the Holy Spirit, but also the acts of the exalted King. Luke sets out to answer the question Jesus's followers were asking themselves once Jesus ascended: "What about the kingdom now?"

The resurrection and ascension of Jesus are not the end of the kingdom but the climax of his inauguration ceremony. Now the Holy Spirit has been poured out, and the apostles are to create, through the Word and the Holy Spirit, kingdom communities. This kingdom message must be declared in every place (Jerusalem, Judea and Samaria, and the end of the earth). Acts is about King Jesus and his power as the exalted Lord now. As Thompson says, "The focus here is not on his 'absence' and consequent 'inactivity,' but rather on the 'place' from which Jesus rules for the rest of Acts."[4] The kingdom story continues through the community of the King.

The kingdom does not disappear in Acts. Acts is the story of the spread of the kingdom. But how can the kingdom spread when Christ is gone? As the exalted and risen Lord, he authorizes his disciples through the Holy Spirit to spread the message of the kingdom. In the kingdom, the risen Lord gives his power to his people, and they spread the message of the King to every place. This is why the book of Acts ends with Paul imprisoned in Rome proclaiming the good news of the kingdom. Acts is not about Paul; it's about the spread of the kingdom.

The Pauline Epistles

Like Acts, some assume kingdom themes are muted in Paul's epistles. True, the phrase "kingdom of God," or variants of it, occurs only eight times in Paul's literature (Rom. 14:17; 1 Cor. 4:20; 6:9–10; 15:24, 50; Gal. 5:21; Col. 4:11; 2 Thess. 1:5). Even the truncated "kingdom" (without the modifier "of God") brings the total to sixteen times in Paul's letters. Consider that Paul wrote around 2,800 words in the canon of Scripture; references to the kingdom appear less than 1 percent of the time.

Maybe Paul dropped the kingdom concept because he was ministering to Gentiles? Was he contextualizing the gospel Jesus preached because he had a new audience? This can't be; as we have just seen, Luke concludes his entire two-volume work with Paul preaching the "kingdom of God" from prison in Rome. Furthermore, we have seen consistently that *kingdom* concerns three loci: power, people, and place.

If we understand the kingdom in this way, then Paul's letters are

---

4. Thompson, *Acts of the Risen Lord Jesus*, 49.

kingdom *dispatches.* He writes *of* Christ the King, *to* the people of the King, in the current manifestation of the kingdom, the church. If Jesus is the composer of the kingdom symphony, then Paul is the conductor who keeps the ensemble in tune with the composer's initial intentions.[5] Paul is simply working out the implications of the kingship of Christ.

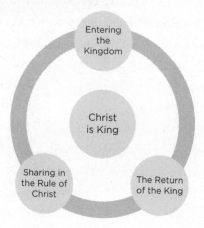

Christ Is King

In Paul's letters there are two hymns famous for their high and lofty language about Christ: Colossians 1:15–20 and Philippians 2:6–11. Paul's language in both hymns is situated in the cultural context of praising kings, emperors, and rulers.[6] Therefore, Paul's theology is centered on Christ as the messianic King. This theology grounds all of Paul's instructions on the community of the King. Because Christ has been crowned as the King, the community needs encouragement to live as citizens of a new city. Thus, the kingdom is the gravitational force to all of Paul's theology and instructions.

---

5. I heard N. T. Wright say this on video at some point.
6. The genesis of this material came from Joshua W. Jipp, *Christ Is King: Paul's Royal Ideology* (Minneapolis, MN: Fortress Press, 2015), 79.

Just before Paul breaks into his poetic section in Colossians 1, he speaks of God, who sent to deliver us from the domain of darkness and transfer us into "the kingdom of his beloved Son" (Col. 1:13). Like a good king, the royal Son liberates his subjects from evil. He has delivered us from the "domain" of darkness and brought us into the "kingdom." Two locale words are put in parallel here. The King through his power (on the cross) has rescued a people (us) and brought us into his place (kingdom). Paul then begins the hymn and depicts the Son using two images: the Son is the image of God and the firstborn of creation (Col. 1:15).

Kings in the ancient world were understood to be living images of the gods. Paul's reference to the image of God is also reminiscent of Adam and Eve, who were made in the image of God and sent out to maintain the divine order of God's creation. Jesus is also the firstborn, which means that (1) he owns all creation, and (2) he rules all creation (Col. 1:16). Not only is the Son the Creator; he is before all things, and in him all things hold together (Col. 1:17).

Paul portrays the Son not only as *like* the kings of the ancient world, but greater than, before, and therefore supreme above them. A new King has arrived. If the Son is the head/ruler of all of creation who establishes divine harmony across the land, then he is also the head of his church (Col. 1:18). He has regal authority over his assembly.[7]

The point is that Paul praises Jesus as the King of the earth. He is the one who delivers his people from his enemies and transfers them to their home. But he is the King not only of the earth but of the universe. He owns and rules all of creation. Therefore, Christ's kingship is cosmic in scope. The King's goal is to establish harmony and security for the world through his people so that they can live

---

7. Ibid., 113.

the good life under his rule. Just as Christ is the King of the universe, so he is the head of the church.

This royal victory is expanded in another one of Paul's hymns, where he explains exactly *how* Christ was crowned as King (Phil. 2:6–11). Here Paul presents Christ as a royal figure who refuses to exploit his equality with God and thereby receives divine honor.[8] Although Christ is "in the form of God," like other rulers and kings in the ancient world, and has "equality with God" (Phil. 2:6), he redefines royal authority by not taking advantage of this status. He accepts public humiliation, taking the form of a slave and submitting to the cross (Phil. 2:8).

The King of heaven was crucified for challenging the king of the earth, Rome. In response, God exalts him to the highest place and gives him the name that is above every name, that every knee should bow in heaven and on earth (Phil. 2:9–10). No conclusion could be clearer about Christ's royal status. Paul draws a comparison here between Christ and the Roman emperors but argues that Christ conquers through sacrifice. If Colossians explains the *extent* of Christ's kingship, then Philippians gives the *means* by which Christ is declared to be King. Jesus's crown is bestowed on him because of the cross.

The point of this brief survey on Paul's two hymns is to show that when Paul praises Christ, he uses royal terminology. For Paul, the kingdom theme has not been put aside. He paints Christ as the King who rules over his whole creation and his community. He has rescued us from darkness; he is the image of God, the firstborn of creation, before all things, and the head of his church. Philippians explains that this came about because he conquered on the cross. He did not exploit his equality with God but humbled himself and therefore was exalted.

---

8. Ibid., 127.

Christ the King is the center of Paul's theology; preaching him is the means of forming the kingdom people. Yet this power of the King, for Paul, as in the Gospels, is showcased in suffering. The King of the universe humbled himself, and this reality characterizes life in this world for his people.

Entering the Kingdom

Paul also provides the answer for how the kingdom community enters into the realm of this King. His epistle to Rome joins the kingship of Christ with the concept of justice. Ancient kings were to enact justice for their people—in both salvation and judgment—and Romans is a long reflection and defense of the justice of God. Paul begins Romans by describing the gospel as a kingly message. Paul depicts himself as being "set apart for the gospel of God" (Rom. 1:1).

This gospel focuses on God's Son descended from David (Rom. 1:1–4). His Davidic descent makes him the rightful King of God's people on earth; his resurrection makes him the rightful King of heaven. This gospel concerns the kingship of Christ through and through. In these opening words, Paul links the gospel with the justice of God: "For in [the gospel] the righteousness of God is revealed from faith for faith" (Rom. 1:17). The rest of Romans in many ways is an explanation of how the gospel reveals the justice of God.

A key text in Romans, 3:21–26, helps explain how the justice of God is revealed and how his community enters into this new realm. According to Romans 3, the justice of God is revealed through Christ the King. God pours out wrath against sin and saves the righteous through the righteousness of the King. Romans 1–3 explains at length that there is no one righteous, not one. So the Son had to absorb the wrath of God against sin. Through substitution, he provided a way for all who have faith in the Messiah to be made right with

God. Faith in the King is the access code to this community. Now the people of God have hope because of the King's work (Romans 5–8). The King has enacted a new law—not a law of sin and death, but a law of Spirit and life. A new era has dawned in which they live by the Spirit and are heirs of the kingdom; here they will be glorified with Christ the King.

Paul's argument in Romans concerns how the King brings justice through his sacrifice and how his people enter this rule through allegiance to this King. God is eternally just because he has demonstrated his justice in the sending of the King as a propitiation for sins. At the cross, all people can come to the King and benefit from his righteous rule over his people. They will do so only by faith in the Messiah because justice is put in right balance in the Messiah. Faith is the way to enter the kingdom.

Paul does not mute kingdom language; he employs it in a roundabout way to explain how the gospel and justice connect. He provides a deeper perspective on the inner working of the kingdom. The kingdom, faith, sin, propitiation, and justice are all part of the same narrative.

Sharing in the Rule of the King

Paul's theology of Christ's kingship is also meant to encourage his readers to share in the rule of Christ. He does this in many ways, telling them to be willing to suffer like their King, to work with their hands, to love one another, and to prefer one another. One thread that ties many of his letters together is the theme of unity. Because the King is bringing peace to the cosmos, Jews and Gentiles are to be a small but tangible picture of this peace. Christ shares his rule with his subjects and gives his Spirit to them so they can participate in his mission.

Paul encourages unity in his kingdom dispatches because of the unity of the Godhead.[9] In Ephesians 4 Paul exhorts those in Ephesus to make every effort to maintain the unity of the Spirit through the bond of peace. Kings in the ancient Near East were praised for bringing peace to people. Accordingly, Paul calls for "one body and one Spirit . . . one hope . . . one Lord, one faith, one baptism, one God and Father of all, who is over all and through all and in all" (Eph. 4:4–7).

He then marries the visible unity of the church to the spatial movement of Christ, speaking of Christ's ascent and descent where he conquered all those who opposed them. Like conquering kings of the ancient world, he brought many captives and spoils of war before the people as he returned to the city (Eph. 4:8–10). However, in Ephesians, the gifts he bestows on his people—apostles, prophets, evangelists, pastors, and teachers—are to equip the saints for the hard work of reaching unity in Christ (Eph. 4:11–13).

So for Paul, the kingship of Christ is tied to the unity of his people in the communities in which they are formed. The kingdom people are raised with the King to rule with the King. Therefore, their gatherings become embassies of the kingdom. For too long the church and the kingdom have seemed at odds, but as we begin to see how Paul ties kingship to his dispatches, we realize the two are inseparable.[10]

The Return of the King

While the King has ascended, one of Paul's main emphases in his letters is that the King will return. Two of Paul's earliest letters, those to the Thessalonians, encourage the church toward hopeful holiness in the midst of hardship, because Christ the King is coming back. The kingdom citizens are comforted by, not fearful of, the day of the Lord (1 Thess. 4:18; 5:8–11), because at the coming of the King they will go out to meet him, celebrating the destruction

---

9. See Philemon, Galatians, and 1 Corinthians for other letters that focus on unity.
10. I am not asserting that the church and the kingdom are equivalent.

of their enemies. The description Paul gives in 1 Thessalonians 4:16 of this return is telling:

> The Lord himself will descend from heaven with a cry of command, with the voice of an archangel, and with the sound of the trumpet of God. And the dead in Christ will rise first.

Most of these images are descriptions of war. The cry of command is reminiscent of God's rebuke of his enemies when he comes to deliver them in the Old Testament. The voice of the archangel also recalls visions of God, accompanied by his angels, fighting on behalf of his people (Zech. 14:1–5). The trumpet is a battle summons; it also declares the victory and power of God.

This imagery gives the impression of an imperial visitation, the return of the king to his city, his people at his side. So while the kingship of Christ has been inaugurated, it has not been consummated yet. He has been crowned and exalted at the right hand of God, but he has not returned yet. Paul comforts the Thessalonians with the sure return of the King but also encourages them to a life of holiness and steadfastness in the meantime (2 Thess. 2:15). Paul views Jesus through the lens of kingship, and this provokes the kingdom communities to hope, patience, and unity.

The Kingdom in Paul

In his letters, Paul isn't contextualizing Jesus's kingdom message as much as he is extending the imagery of the kingdom. He presents an in-depth picture of Christ as King for the people the Spirit is forming. His aim is that they live rightly under this rule. This kingship was accomplished *through* the justice of God, and *for* the unity of his people; it will be consummated *when* Christ the King comes back.

Paul's fundamental conviction is that Christ has been crowned King of the universe through his crucifixion and resurrection. The only way to participate in this kingdom is through faith. Faith, not works, is the access code to this new city, and when people enter they share in the rule of Christ. The community is also to wait expectantly for the King to return.

Paul writes to the people of the King, who are gathered together, about the rule of Christ. In one sense, nothing has changed from the garden, for Christ's kingdom has always been about the King's power over the King's people in the King's place. In another sense everything has changed, for *the* King has come, and now he is forming his community.

The General Epistles

The General Epistles continue the theme of the community of the kingdom. Although Hebrews, James, 1–2 Peter, and Jude were not collected and disseminated together, they do have coherent themes.[11] Each is written from a vertical and horizontal worldview: because of Christ's enthronement as King and Lord (vertical), community life implications arise (horizontal). The conviction of all these authors was that the kingdom communities were living in the last days because King Jesus had arrived and been raised from the dead.

HEBREWS: THE PRIEST-KING AND THE COMMUNITY

Hebrews looks to Christ as the Priest King. The opening lines speak of the Son as the one "appointed the heir of all things, through whom also he created the world. . . . He sat down at the right hand of the Majesty on high" (Heb. 1:2–3). These are kingly, enthronement images. The theme of the kingship of Christ remains with the title

---

11. Hebrews was usually placed in the Pauline canon although the authorship was always debated.

"Son," which plays a major role in Hebrews (Heb. 1:2, 5, 8; 3:6; 4:14; 5:5, 8; 6:6; 7:3, 28; 10:29). In the Old Testament, Israel was depicted as God's son. More specifically, the Davidic king is appointed God's son and the firstborn (2 Sam. 7:14; Ps. 89:27). Jesus is thus the true Davidic King in Hebrews.

But of the Son he says,

> "Your throne, O God, is forever and ever,
>> the scepter of uprightness is the scepter of your
>> kingdom. . . .

And . . .

> "Sit at my right hand,
>> until I make your enemies a footstool for your feet."
>> (Heb. 1:8–13)

In the passage above, Psalm 45—originally about the Davidic king— has been fulfilled in Jesus Christ the King. This kingship motif continues in Hebrews 7 when Melchizedek is introduced as a priest and king (v. 1). Jesus comes as the new "king of righteousness" and "king of peace" (v. 2). So Hebrews presents Jesus as the King by labeling him as "the Son" and "the king of righteousness."

Hebrews focuses not only on the *power* of the King but also on the *place* of the kingdom. Great focus is placed upon the "rest" the King provides and the heavenly nature of the kingdom (Heb. 3:7– 4:13). All who believe enter the kingly rest (Heb. 4:3). While this rest is connected with Canaan (and Genesis 2), it also supersedes it, for it is an eternal rest (Heb. 4:8). Belief in the power of the King enables one to enter the eternal land of rest.

Finally, Hebrews also warns and encourages the *people* of the kingdom. They are exhorted in light of Jesus's superiority and the heavenly nature of the kingdom not to fall away but to continue to consider their faithful Priest King. Like the saints of old, they are to look forward to a heavenly city and recognize that they are exiles and aliens on this earth. The earthly kingdoms will pass away, but Christ has initiated a kingdom that will never pass away. They need to draw near to God through the Priest King, who is over the house of God (Heb. 10:22), and consider how to stir up one another to the deeds of the heavenly kingdom: love and good works. Hebrews directs our gaze to Christ the King, the people of the King, and their everlasting heavenly kingdom.

JAMES: NEW WISDOM

The epistle of James, like the Wisdom Literature, focuses on life in the kingdom. How are people to live now that the King has come? The brother of Jesus centers on Jesus Christ as Lord (or King) through whom all wisdom flows. Five times in James, lordship is ascribed to Jesus (James 1:1; 2:1 [2x]; 5:7, 8), and this becomes the basis for his concern for righteous living.

Wisdom comes through living a new life where fighting does not define relationships (James 4:1–3), where speech is used to heal and not divide (James 3:1–12), where no partiality is shown (James 2:1–13), where people are hearers and doers of the word (James 1:19–26), and where the difficulties of this present life are preparatory for the crown of life (James 1:2–4, 12).

Just as in Paul's writings, the kingdom citizens begin to share in the rule of the King, but they do so in following Jesus's example of humility, love, and kindness. James's entreaties about life in the kingdom flow from his conviction that we are citizens (people) in community (place) under the lordship of Jesus (power). Trials and tribulations will come; although the kingdom is already here, it is still not consummated.

Peter and Jude: The End Is at Hand

As we move through the Bible, a temporal development occurs. The emphasis of Peter's and Jude's epistles can be captured in this phrase: "The end of all things is at hand" (1 Pet. 4:7). Although Christ has accomplished all, the fulfillment has not been realized. The community of the King is to live out their new identity in this in-between time as elect exiles—a "chosen race, a royal priesthood, a holy nation" (1 Pet. 2:9).

They are sharers in the rule of the King, and they are being built up and have an imperishable inheritance (1 Pet. 1:4). They are living stones being built into "a spiritual house" (1 Pet. 2:5). "Spiritual" does not mean nonphysical but rather points to the new temple and the new creation. They are to be built up as a community into a place— a house. The language certainly comes from the words Jesus said to Peter about being the rock upon which his church will be built (Matt. 16:18). Because they are God's temple, they are to contend for the faith (Jude 3).

In order to be built up in such a way, they are to have ordered households. Household codes are the instruction manuals for the kingdom. The elect exiles' interpersonal relationships are the bedrock of a well-ordered society. While household management advice was common in the ancient world, at least two differences stand out in the biblical presentation.

First, Peter, like Paul, addresses not only the socially dominant but also the "subordinate" groups, treating them as moral agents who are capable and responsible to the exhortations. Both those in dominant and subordinate roles would have heard the commands given to the respective groups. Peter thus indicates that in the kingdom all are viewed as agents and participants in God's redemption.

Second, Peter, like Paul, bases these instructions on the lordship

of Christ. Peter compares the suffering of slaves with the suffer-
ings of Christ (1 Pet. 2:18–25). The way to power and unity is
through the humility exemplified in Christ on the cross. Peter and
Paul in the household codes form the interpersonal relationships of
kingdom citizens so that the city might flourish as the citizens treat
one another respectfully and in love.

The emphasis here is on *people* and the *places* they create through
their social interaction under the *lordship* of Christ. The household
codes (1 Pet. 3:1–7) are meant to shine forth to the world the peaceful
rest of the coming and the present kingdom.

Summary: The Kingdom in Acts and the Epistles

The Gospels end with Christ the King resurrected and ascended. The
rest of the New Testament answers the question, "What happens in
the kingdom now that the King is gone?" The focus does not turn
away from Jesus but seizes upon his exalted and risen status, the work
of his Spirit and Word, and the formation of his community. King
Jesus is now creating his community from all nations. The church is
to be salt and light, for they are elect exiles and servants of the King
on an earth that needs to hear the kingdom announcement.

Thus, the kingdom story is not dropped, deemphasized, or even
recontextualized in Acts and the Epistles. Nor does the kingdom
become an abstract notion of sovereignty. Rather, the eyes of faith
move from seeing Jesus on earth to seeing him in heaven. The King
has ascended; these letters help the King's people learn to live in
community, experiencing the King's activity in and through them
by his Spirit.

However, everything is still not right. In Corinth, people are still
suing one another and fighting about whom to follow. In Galatia,
Jews and Gentiles are not getting along. In Ephesus, there are leadership problems. In Thessalonica, there is persecution. The King reigns,

but not all of his enemies have been crushed underfoot. We sense the tension—the end is near but not completely here. The community of believers is encouraged to live in holiness but with their eyes raised and looking for the King's return. If you listen closely, you can hear the sound of the archangel saying the time is near.

6

Revelation

Achieving the Kingdom Goal

Revelation tells the story of a fallen tree burning in an eternal flame. The image is an apocalyptic vision of a destroyed kingdom juxtaposed with a victorious kingdom. In a similar way, Percy Shelley, in his sonnet "Ozymandias," writes about a traveler seeing a statue in ruin and resting in the desert. The head of this figurine is described as

> Half sunk, a shattered visage lies, whose frown,
> And wrinkled lip, and sneer of cold command.

On the pedestal of the statue are the words,

> My name is Ozymandias, King of Kings:
> Look on my Works, ye Mighty, and despair![1]

---

1. Percy Bysshe Shelley, *The Works of Percy Bysshe Shelley in Verse and Prose*, vol. 1 (London: Reeves & Turner, 1880), 376.

Ozymandias is the Greek name for the Egyptian pharaoh Ramesses II. Shelley's poem speaks to the inevitable decline of all leaders and empires in contrast to their pretentions for greatness. The book of Revelation also juxtaposes the pride of the kingdoms of mankind with their eventual "colossal wreck, boundless and bare."[2] Each kingdom that sets itself up against God's kingdom will be left shattered. Only one kingdom will remain.

The canon of Scripture culminates with the cry of an archangel.[3] Revelation describes an apocalyptic battle between the city of Babylon and the city of God. The kingdom was launched in Genesis, challenged from the very beginning, and then consummated in Revelation. From the garden, through Abraham and David, to Jesus, to the church, we are desperate to know how the story will end. Will the people of God be rescued? Will their King return? Will their cities be rebuilt? What will happen to the enemies of the King? Will the crucified and ascended King reveal himself again?

While the King plants his foot on the earth in the Gospels, the rest of the New Testament makes evident that all is not as it should be. The revelation to John on the island of Patmos concludes the story in a series of visions. The visions come in the form of letters to churches, bizarre narratives, and musical poetry, all with an apocalyptic focus—that is, pulling back the curtain of history. John's vista is filled with dragons, beasts, blood, scorpions, and war.

Although modern readers regularly get confused by this writing style, "the goal of apocalyptic literature is not prediction, but unmasking—unveiling the realities around us for what they really are."[4]

---

2. Ibid.

3. Or as Barker writes, "It is significant that the Bible begins (Genesis 1–2) and ends (Revelation 19–22) with royal motifs." Kenneth L. Barker, "The Scope and Center of Old and New Testament Theology and Hope," in *Dispensationalism, Israel and the Church: The Search for Definition* (Grand Rapids, MI: Zondervan, 1992), 306.

4. James K. A. Smith, *Desiring the Kingdom: Worship, Worldview, and Cultural Formation* (Grand Rapids, MI: Baker Academic, 2009), 92.

Apocalyptic literature is thus a way of seeing; a way of discerning God's invading power in human events both presently and typologically in the future. Revelation is a book about the past, present, and future. It is an encouragement to Christians of all ages who wonder how the King will complete this kingdom story promised to Adam, Abraham, and David. John reveals the supernatural nature of this battle that has been waging between the seed of mankind and the seed of the Serpent from the time of Adam and Eve. The dragon and the woman are at war.

To use another image, the tree that is attempting to grow and fill the earth will meet the opposition of axes, fire, and rock, but God Almighty guarantees he will build a protective hedge around this tree so that it will fill the entire earth. Revelation continues the trio of kingdom themes that were inaugurated in the creation of the world, arguing that the *kingdom goal is now achieved*. John does so by revealing what is behind the scenes from multiple viewpoints (what some call "progressive recapitulation"). Therefore, we will also identify the consummation of the kingdom through recapitulating descriptions. The power of God and the Lamb is manifested in the judgment of the kingdom's enemies. The people of the King are shielded and protected. The place of the kingdom is cleansed and prepared so that they might live with him forever and ever. Before this can happen, the dragon must be slain by the Lamb.

Law	Reviving hope in the kingdom
Prophets	Foreshadowing the kingdom
Writings	Life in the kingdom
Gospels	Embodying the kingdom
Acts and Epistles	Kingdom community
Revelation	**Achieving the kingdom goal**

The Power of God and the Lamb

As Richard Bauckham notes, "The role of Christ in Revelation is to establish God's kingdom on the earth: in the words of 11:15, to turn 'the kingdom of the world' (currently ruled by evil) into 'the kingdom of our Lord and his Messiah.'"[5] So how does this happen?

In Revelation it is by the power of God and the Lamb. The power is displayed *through* the conquest of their enemies and *by* a sacrificial death.[6] The power of God and the Lamb is manifested in (1) John's visions of the worship in the temple; (2) the opening of the scroll; (3) the unleasing of the seals, trumpets, and bowls; and (4) in the conquering of Babylon, the dragon, and the kings of the earth.

In Revelation 4, John sees God seated upon the throne as King (v. 2). The four living creatures surround the King and bow down to him (v. 8). They worship God because he is Creator—and therefore King—of all things (v. 11). This heavenly court is the place from which judgment against the kingdoms of the earth will flow. The rule is manifested in the opening of the scroll. The scroll is the instrument of judgment on the enemies of the King.

Yet no one can open the scroll except the Lion of the tribe of Judah, the Root of David (Rev. 5:5). He is also a Lamb who has been slain (Rev. 5:6). By juxtaposing Lion and Lamb, a new symbol of sacrificial conquest is forged. "In one brilliant stroke," says Robert Mounce, "John portrays the central theme of NT revelation—victory through sacrifice."[7] Throughout the rest of the letter, the Lion is redefined by the Lamb. Subjugation is portrayed through sacrifice. The

---

5. Richard Bauckham, *The Theology of the Book of Revelation* (Cambridge, UK: Cambridge University Press, 1993), 67.

6. John begins by describing Jesus as the firstborn of the dead and the ruler of the kings of the earth (Rev. 1:5). This language of the "firstborn of the dead" echoes what was said about Jesus in Colossians where the firstborn receives the inheritance. Jesus is also "the ruler of kings" of the earth establishing him as the highest King, the King of kings. John is then caught up into heaven and sees a throne, cherubim, and seven torches (Rev. 1:10–20). John knew where he was; he was in the temple. The temple was the house of the high King.

7. Robert H. Mounce, *The Book of Revelation* (Grand Rapids, MI: Eerdmans, 1997), 132.

slain Lamb is now and forever more. As Boring says, "Crucifixion was not . . . superseded by the resurrection and exaltation; it is the definitive act which stamps its character on the identity of Christ."[8] This Lamb conquers through sacrifice (Rev. 3:21; 5:5; 17:14), as do those who follow him (Rev. 2:7, 11, 17, 26; 3:5, 12, 21; 12:11; 15:2; 21:7).

When the Lamb opens the seal, he unleashes destruction on the earth. This is a de-creation, contrasted with God's work in Genesis. Human rebellion spurs on the de-creation, the natural consequence of snubbing the Creator and King of the universe. The King of heaven and the Lamb pour out their wrath on all of humankind, focusing on the kings of the earth:

> The kings of the earth and the great ones and the generals and the rich and the powerful, and everyone, slave and free, hid themselves in the caves and among the rocks of the mountains, calling to the mountains and rocks, "Fall on us and hide us from the face of him who is seated on the throne, and from the wrath of the Lamb." (Rev. 6:15–16)

No one can stand against the Lamb's cleansing of the earth. The section in Revelation 12–14 zooms in on this apocalyptic battle between the citizens of the kingdom of God and those of the kingdom of Satan. It begins with the birth of Christ (Rev. 12:5) and walks through the age of the church, revealing that the Devil (dragon) himself is the deeper source of destruction and war. War arises in heaven between the angels and the dragon (Rev. 12:7), and the dragon is defeated and thrown down to the earth. A loud voice in heaven says, "Now the salvation and the power and the kingdom of our God and the authority of his Christ have come" (Rev. 12:10). It is by the *power* of God and Christ that the kingdom comes.

---

8. M. Eugene Boring, *Revelation*, Interpretation (Louisville, KY: Westminster John Knox, 2011), 109.

This power is also vividly illustrated in the bowls poured out on the earth in Revelation 15–16. Those who conquered the beast sing the song of the Lamb, praising him for his great deeds, the glory of his name, and his righteous acts (Rev. 15:3–4). These bowls are depicted as the bowls of the wrath of God (Rev. 16:1), and they are dispensed upon the earth. At the seventh bowl, the declaration goes out, "It is done!" (Rev. 16:17). But it is not quite done in one sense, because John is still going to give two more visions: one of the fall of Babylon (Revelation 17–19) and the other of the great consummation (Revelation 21–22). Babylon is personified as a woman, a prostitute with whom the kings of the earth have committed sexual immorality (Rev. 17:1–2). Although she glorified herself, the mighty Lord God judges her and the kings of the earth who committed sexual immorality with her (Rev. 18:18–19). In the end, a great millstone is tied to Babylon, and she sinks to the bottom of the ocean.

Again, it is proclaimed, "Salvation and glory and power belong to our God" (Rev. 19:1). The repetition of this phrase throughout the book displays the focus on the power of the King of the kingdom. Victory is achieved through sacrifice and judgment.

The People of God

As we see the immense power of the Lamb in Revelation, we are comforted that he wields this power *for* the people of God and the glory of his name. More specifically, the people of God are protected from the kingdom of man, the second death, and the wrath of the Lamb. In the midst of chaos and destruction, God casts his protective wings over his people. God protects his own tree but levels the sapling kingdoms of the earth.[9] The interludes in Revelation between

---

9. John begins writing to the seven churches that Christ has made a kingdom of priests (Rev. 1:6). Here John equates the people and the kingdom. The people themselves comprise and are described as a kingdom.

the sixth plague and the seventh plague impress upon readers not only the power of this King of kings, but his power meted out for the protection of his own people.

While Revelation is filled with carcasses, valleys of the dead, and bloodstained streets, the interludes provide respite where the people of God are marked out and sheltered. The people of the Lamb are shielded from the wrath of the Lamb; they are "sealed" in safety. The 144,000 from every tribe of Israel are sheltered. The people then cry out that salvation belongs to God, who sits on the throne, and to the Lamb (Rev. 7:10). This statement of praise links the idea of the power of God (and of the Lamb) with the protection of his people. The 144,000 are sheltered in the presence of the Lamb; he safeguards them from sin, death, and eternal destruction. Indeed, he wipes away all their tears (Rev. 7:15–17).

Between the sixth and seventh trumpets, a second interlude again views the 144,000 but with different symbols. Revelation 11 speaks of the two witnesses who are protected in the midst of suffering. Like the 144,000, these two represent the people of God. John receives a measuring rod, and he measures those who are worshiping in the temple to protect them (Rev. 11:1). Those who oppose the two witnesses will be destroyed with fire.

While the Beast will conquer and kill the two witnesses for a time, after three and a half days the breath of life from God enters them and they rise to their feet (Rev. 11:11). This recalls the breath of God that enters mankind in Genesis. It signifies God re-creating the earth with his resurrected people. While God is de-creating through judgment, he is also re-creating through resurrection life. In the midst of the hurricane of destruction in Revelation, the people are safeguarded in the eye of the storm, sealed by the blood of the Lamb.

In the last battle (Revelation 17–19) the people of God are again preserved through the destruction of the city of Babylon. When God's people see what has become of Babylon, the strutting, violent, and immoral city, they cry out, "Hallelujah! Salvation and glory and power belong to our God. . . . Hallelujah! The smoke from her goes up forever and ever" (Rev. 19:1–3). They praise the Lord God because he reigns and the marriage supper of the Lamb has come.

Revelation 21–22 declares at the consummation that the dwelling place of God is with man: "He will dwell with them, and they will be his people" (Rev. 21:3). The purpose of this manifestation of power is the reunion of God and man. The kingdom in Revelation is not only the power of the King; his power is manifested as the protection of his people and the judgment of his opponents.

The Place of God

People regularly overlook the location of the kingdom in the biblical text, but it is always present—Revelation included. As Ladd notes, "the central theme of the book of Revelation is the establishment of the Kingdom of God on the earth."[10] Revelation was written not just for modern readers; its original recipients were the struggling churches in AD 90. The seven churches John addresses are embassies of the kingdom. They are lampstands in the house of God (Rev. 1:13).

Through warnings and encouragements, John is attempting to establish these churches as places where the King can manifest his rule. If they conquer, they will be made pillars in the temple of God: "Never shall he go out of it, and I will write on him the name of my God, and the name of the city of my God, the new Jerusalem, which comes down from my God out of heaven, and my own new name" (Rev. 3:12). Here, the risen Christ speaks of the people of God as the

---

10. G. E. Ladd, *A Commentary on the Revelation of John* (Grand Rapids, MI: Eerdmans, 1972), 281.

place of God. They are pillars in the temple; they are the New Jerusalem. The kingdom concerns both people and place.

The spatial nature of the kingdom is also evidenced in the triadic series of the seals, the trumpets, and the bowls. These destructions are regularly poured out on earth, sea, and sun. This includes the seals (Rev. 6:4, 8, 12), the trumpets (Rev. 8:6–12; 10:2; 12:4; 14:14–20), and the bowls, which likewise are poured out on earth, sea, rivers, sun, air, and the throne of the Beast (Rev. 16:1–17).

Using apocalyptic imagery, John's visions show judgment coming upon both the people and the place where they dwell. Again and again it is earth, sea, air, waters, and sun that are destroyed. These places are destroyed because they are the dwelling place of those who stand against the Lord's Anointed One. As we saw in Matthew, the King of heaven brings his rule upon the kingdoms of the earth.

The climax of all this judgment is poured out on a *place*: the city of Babylon. Revelation 17–19 depicts the city as it falls. Why does John personify the last great enemy of the kingdom as a city and a prostitute? Precisely because the cities of the earth have set themselves up against the kingdom of Christ. So the Lamb brings Babylon to utter destruction. This is instructive for our understanding of the kingdom; the antonym to the kingdom is a place.

Babylon, the city of earth, represents all the cities opposed to the reign of God. The city turns from a place of glory to a dwelling place for demons, for every unclean and detestable beast (Rev. 18:2). Her wealth is laid to waste, and judgment falls upon her. Then God establishes his own kingdom—his own city—in Revelation 21–22. A new heaven and a new earth are made, and the holy city, the New Jerusalem, comes down from heaven (Rev. 21:1–2). The New Jerusalem is described in great detail. It has great high walls, radiance like jasper, and strong foundations, and its length and width are even, and the city is filled with jewels. Babylon is contrasted to Jerusalem, two cities—two *places*. In one very real sense, the entire book of Revelation could be summarized as the warring of these two cities.

As Revelation comes to a close, the good kingdom is pictured as a metropolis. One of the Spirit's last visions to John is a picture of the bride, the wife of the Lamb (Rev. 21:9). We expect to see a multitude of people as before, but John sees a city: "And he carried me away in the Spirit to a great, high mountain, and showed me the holy city Jerusalem coming down out of heaven from God" (Rev. 21:10). At the center of this city is a throne. The New Jerusalem is a paradise, a holy city, and a temple all at once. God has already declared at the end of Isaiah, "For behold, I create new heavens / and a new earth, / and the former things shall not be remembered / or come into mind" (Isa. 65:17).

The kingdom concept in Revelation is not just about the power of God, but the power of God displayed for the sake of his people to establish them in their new home. For Israelites this makes plain sense; this is exactly what was promised to both Abraham and David. But the only one worthy to undertake this project is the Lamb who was slain. As VanGemeren writes, "The Bible begins with the account of creation (Gen 1–2) and ends with a description of a more glorious creation (Rev 21–22). Between these accounts lies the story of redemption."[11]

The Tree of Life

The goal of the kingdom achieved in Revelation is described as a city, a people, and a conquering King. From the throne of this King comes a river with water (Rev. 22:1–2; think Gen. 2:10 and Ezek. 47:1–12), and on either side of the river is the tree of life with its twelve kinds of fruit for the healing of nations.

---

11. Willem VanGemeren, *The Progress of Redemption: The Story of Salvation from Creation to the New Jerusalem* (Grand Rapids, MI: Baker Academic, 1996), 40.

As Genesis began with the garden and the tree of life, now Revelation closes with a garden city and a tree that heals all the nations. Genesis began with a marriage; so also Revelation finishes with the wedding feast of the Lamb. The twelve kinds of fruit harken us back to the promise made to Abraham's offspring, that they would bring blessings to the whole world. They are the chosen people through whom God established his kingdom.

The Messiah has come to fulfill the destiny of Israel's seed in feeding all the nations. Israel's hopes were too small. The tree that bore their king transformed into a source of life for the entire world. Streaming into the city are the kings of the earth who come to give their glory to the King of kings, who reigns over all people.

The tree of the knowledge of good and evil seemed to send the kingdom plan on a downward spiral, but it was through the tree of the cross that the kingdom was fulfilled. Now the tree of life consummates the kingdom story started so long ago. The dragon is slain; the Lamb has won; the people are free; they are home.[12]

Summary: The Kingdom in the New Testament

The New Testament begins with the birth of a child. The true King arrives, and he embodies the kingdom:

> For to us a child is born,
>> to us a son is given;
> and the government shall be upon his shoulder,
>> and his name shall be called
> Wonderful Counselor, Mighty God,
>> Everlasting Father, Prince of Peace.
> Of the increase of his government and of peace

---

12. As Augustine said, "He endured death as a lamb; he devoured it as lion." Augustine, Sermon 375A: On the Sacraments (397), *Works of Saint Augustine*, 10:330.

> there will be no end,
> on the throne of David and over his kingdom,
>> to establish it and to uphold it
> with justice and with righteousness
>> from this time forth and forevermore.
> The zeal of the LORD of hosts will do this. (Isa. 9:6–7)

But then this Prince of Peace is crucified and leaves the earth. Yet the kingdom story is not over; it is just beginning. Christ conquers and is crowned through his death and resurrection. God sends his Spirit to fill his church to carry the message of justice and righteousness to the whole world. The kingdom community is now formed.

Just as God began the creation of his kingdom with words in Genesis, so he instructs his disciples to proclaim the King and the kingdom through words. At the center of this kingdom plan stand the new people of God, who are created by the Word. God called out not a group of individuals, but a community. Paul speaks of this community as confounding the heavenly beings (Eph. 3:10). It is through the church that people get a glimpse of the kingdom.

Interestingly, both Paul and Jesus run to agricultural imagery to depict the work of their ministry. In the kingdom parables, Jesus uses the imagery of a sower who went out to sow (Matt. 13:3). Later, Jesus identifies both his disciples and his words as seeds that go out in the ground (Matt. 13:18, 20). Although many of the words are choked out, others have an effect in the community and produce fruit.

Jesus is establishing his kingdom through his words in people that affect place. Sometimes the seed grows, if it is planted on good soil, but other times it is choked out. Maybe this is why Paul also uses agricultural imagery. In 1 Corinthians 3:6–9 Paul portrays his ministry as planting and others' as watering, but God gives the growth. He goes on to designate the church as God's field and God's building

(1 Cor. 3:9). In 2 Thessalonians Paul speaks of the faith and love of the Thessalonian believers "flourishing," a compound verb transforming it from growth to wonderful growth (2 Thess. 1:3 CSB). In Ephesians 4:15 Paul says we are to "grow" into a holy temple in the Lord.

Both Jesus and Paul picture their ministries as building a tree that will spread its roots deep into the ground—and they do this through words. Words nourish the plants in the soil, and those plants grow up to be strong trees in the kingdom of Christ. Even now God welcomes all to the place that is nourished by the river that flows from the throne of God. In Revelation the kingdom goal is achieved as the tree is planted by the water that is called "life," and the water is as bright as crystal.

Conclusion

Kingdom through Cross

God is King. Perhaps we are prone to think of God as friend, or Father, or as some impersonal force or mystical presence. However, kingship is the root metaphor for the Bible's description of God. This metaphor brings coherence and unity to the rest of the metaphors.

Americans particularly have a hard time with this depiction, because we have rejected the monarchy in our governmental system. I was reminded of the importance of kingship in other nations when I watched the Netflix program *The Crown*, which chronicles the rise of Queen Elizabeth II. In one scene Queen Mary of Teck gives advice to the newly crowned Queen Elizabeth II about her divine calling. She says:

> Monarchy is God's sacred mission to grace and dignify the earth. To give ordinary people an ideal to strive towards, an example of nobility and duty to raise them in their wretched lives. Monarchy is a calling from God. That is why you are crowned in an abbey, not a government building. Why you are anointed, not appointed. It's an archbishop that puts

the crown on your head, not a minister or a public servant. Which means that you are answerable to God in your duty, not the public.[1]

While modern governments don't necessarily need to have a monarchy, the biblical story supports monarchy as God's sacred mission. But if God has always been King, as the Bible claims, then how can kingship be his sacred mission?[2]

The answer is provided through recognizing that God chose to exercise his kingship through his agents. Adam, Abraham, Isaac, and Jacob were to be his kings, but they all failed. So a new and true King is crowned. Through Jesus the Messiah, God reclaims his rule over Israel and the world. But God reclaims his rule paradoxically through the cross.

At times an emphasis on the kingdom displaces or at least shifts attention away from a theology of the cross. It seems that we are prone to speak either of the kingdom or of the cross, unintentionally driving a wedge between the two.[3] However, it is precisely in Jesus's announcement, "The kingdom of God is at hand," that he presupposes the kingdom will be accomplished by his death. The kingdom is not a higher or more important theme than the cross. These two realities are forever joined; separating them is an act of violence.

If the kingdom is the *goal*, then the cross is the *means*. But this

---

1. "Act of God," season 1, episode 4, *The Crown*, directed by Julian Jarrold, produced by Peter Morgan (London: Left Bank Pictures, 2016).

2. There are numerous references that speak of God as the everlasting king. Psalm 45:6 says of God, "Your throne, O God, is forever and ever. / The scepter of your kingdom is a scepter of uprightness." Psalm 93:1–2 says, "The LORD reigns; he is robed in majesty. / . . . Your throne is established from of old; / you are from everlasting." The Lord is called "a great king over all the earth" in Psalm 47:2.

3. Treat argues there are six reasons for this separation: (1) social gospel movement and the conservative response; (2) fragmentation of Scripture; (3) the ditch between biblical studies and systematic theology; (4) the Gospels have been ignored as a source for theology; (5) oversystematized doctrines; (6) misunderstandings about both the kingdom and cross. Jeremy R. Treat, *The Crucified King: Atonement and Kingdom in Biblical and Systematic Theology* (Grand Rapids, MI: Zondervan, 2014), 26–28.

does not mean that the cross simply falls between the ages. Rather, it is the wheel that shifts one age into another; it is the great transition piece, the turn of the ages for the people of God seeking their place. Martin Luther said that the cross must be the test of everything, and that includes a biblical theology of the kingdom. Jesus becomes King *through* the cross.[4] Two final reflections confirm this.

Blood on the Post

First, the cross is a picture of the new exodus. Rabbi Michael Goldberg calls the exodus a "master story" for Jews.[5] It functions as a foundational and fundamental story through which they got their bearings on what God was doing in the world. If this is the case, then we must pause and ask ourselves what the exodus narrative teaches us about the nature of the kingdom. In other words, what happens when the Passover and exodus shape our view of the kingdom story?

The exodus was about the deliverance of the people of Israel from Egypt. They had been enslaved for four hundred years, and then God came to rescue them from the hands of their oppressors. God performed this action by many signs and wonders. The night of the Passover was the last plague, where the Lord showed that he was the one true God by slaying the firstborn of all the Egyptians. In so doing, Pharaoh, the god of Egypt, lost the one who was to inherit his throne.

But God protected his people and the inheritor to *his* throne by

---

4. But what about the resurrection? Is this emphasis on the cross neglecting the vindication of the cross in his resurrection from the dead? For Paul, it seems that to speak about the cross is to speak about the resurrection. They are in some sense the same event, a double-sided saving act. In the same letter Paul says that he decided to know only Christ and his death (1 Cor. 2:12), and he says, "If there is no resurrection of the dead, then not even Christ has been raised. And if Christ has not been raised, then our preaching is in vain" (1 Cor. 15:13–14). Focusing on the cross does not ignore or downplay the resurrection; it assumes and includes it. The resurrection clues God's creatures in on the goal of all creation—new creation. The resurrection is only significant in light of the cross, and the cross is only victorious in view of the raised body of Christ.

5. Michael Goldberg, *Why Should Jews Survive?: Looking Past the Holocaust Toward a Jewish Future* (New York: Oxford University Press, 1996), n.p.

covering them in blood. If they spread blood over their doorposts, the angel of death would pass by them. The goal of this redemption from Egypt was that the people of God could go live in their land and worship God. If the exodus is a master narrative, then it is telling that it was about the power of God, meted out for his people, so they could enter their home. The exodus is an anticipatory act—a shadow—of the coming kingdom. But my focus is on how this redemption came about: blood-covered wood.

Although the Gospel writers don't mention it, when Jesus was dangling on the cross, there must have been blood running down the beams from the lacerations on his back. Blood was a powerful symbol for Jews. At the first Passover, blood was spread over the posts of Israel's doors in the land of Egypt so that the angel of death would pass by and let their firstborn children live. Blood and the exodus were allies. Christ's bloody crucifixion, which took place on the week of Passover, is meant to recall the images and symbols of the exodus story. In the exodus, salvation came through death. So too entry into the new creation comes through blood on wood.

The New Testament authors, from the earliest moments, construed the death of Jesus as the new Passover—the new exodus. In 1 Corinthians 5:7–8 Paul says, "Christ, our Passover lamb, has been sacrificed." All four Gospels set the passion narrative during the Passover feast.

And at the Last Supper Jesus says, "This cup that is poured out for you is the new covenant in my blood" (Luke 22:20). So when the earliest Christians interpreted Jesus's death, they saw it through the lens of the exodus and the Passover. On the cross, Christ rescued them from death and delivered them from slavery. At the cross, the people of God were saved from death, delivered from their sins, and set on the path to return home to their place.

Just as the blood of the Passover lamb was the means of preserving his people from death and covering their sins, so the blood of Jesus on the wooden post rolled out the kingdom plan. On the cross the sign read, "The King of the Jews." There the King was crowned in the most unexpected way.

The exodus and the Passover are the images that early Christian interpreters used to understand the cross. Jesus was enthroned on the cross, and *it is only through the cross that the kingdom comes.* If there had been no blood on the tree, there would be no kingdom. If there had been no death of the Messiah, there would be no deliverance. As Augustine said, "The Lord has established his sovereignty from a tree. Who is it who fights with wood? Christ. From his cross he has conquered kings."[6] The kingdom of God has been established through the cross of Christ by which Jesus's reign is irreversibly fixed on earth as it is in heaven.

Two Destinies

So what are we going to do with this bloody King? Will we accept him or turn from him? Will we seek to construct our own kingdom, or will we submit to his upside-down kingdom? Luke presents this option to us through the two thieves on the cross. Jesus was not the only one crucified the day the sun went dark. There were two other convicts who were ingloriously pinned up alongside Jesus.[7]

For Luke, these are not only historical figures, but literary figures who represent the choices of all mankind. Will they recognize the Messiah through the cross, or will the blood be a hindrance to their sight? One sees; the other is blinded. The cross is the key to this decision.

While the three were heaving for their last fleeting breaths, one of

---

6. Augustine, *Exposition of Psalm 95, Works of Saint Augustine*, 18:425.
7. This imagery was used by Fleming Rutledge, *The Crucifixion: Understanding the Death of Jesus Christ* (Grand Rapids, MI: Eerdmans, 2015), 1.

them called out to Jesus, "Are you not the Christ? Save yourself and us!" (Luke 23:39). He seemed to view the Messiah as a savior of the people—a standard view of the day. But the Jesus he saw seemed like no king. For how could the Messiah be on the cross? The cross was the stumbling block for seeing Jesus as King.

But the other thief asked Jesus to remember him when he came into his kingdom. How could this thief have viewed a bloodied, beaten, and crucified criminal as the kingdom ruler? Maybe he was confused, or delirious.[8] Or maybe he suddenly had insight into the relationship between the kingdom and a crucified Messiah.

In a moment, for this thief, the relationship between the crucified Messiah and kingdom was revealed. The cross is not contrary to this King and kingdom, but the center of it. This King *has* power, but it is a paradoxical power, one of suffering and weakness. Somehow this outcast recognized that despite what he was seeing, this Messiah will come again in power, and the kingdom will be consummated. This King also came to save a people, people like the thief beside him, but if the people reject him they have no place in the kingdom. The kingdom is about the King's people, but they must accept and trust the King on the cross. The cross is the entrance for people to either enter the kingdom or be thrown out forever.

The narrative also reveals that the cross is the entrance to the kingdom place. When the thief asked Jesus to remember him when he came into his kingdom, Jesus answered by telling him about a place: "Today you will be with me in paradise" (Luke 23:43). Luke, at this pivotal moment, joins together the King, paradise, and a decision at the cross. He naturally puts on the cross a conversation about the who, what, and where of the kingdom, because the cross is the center of this kingdom plan.

---

8. See similar questions from Jeremy Treat, *The Crucified King: Atonement and Kingdom in Biblical and Systematic Theology* (Grand Rapids, MI: Zondervan, 2014), 25.

As Ridderbos said, "The kingdom cannot be understood without the cross, nor the cross without the kingdom."[9] The day the new creation began was the day Jesus died. He was strung up as a common criminal on a Roman cross, and history has not been able to ignore what was a regular spectacle of that day. This is because Christians quickly began to interpret his death as the center of their faith. This was no common death but a substitution for the sins of the world. Kingdom and cross go together. Jesus's "main message was the kingdom and his main mission was to go to Golgotha."[10] Kingdom and cross must mutually interpret each other, and they must be kept in the same orbit. As Wright says:

> The fact that the kingdom is redefined by the cross doesn't mean that it isn't still the kingdom. The fact that the cross is the kingdom-bringing event doesn't mean that it isn't still an act of horrible and brutal injustice, on the one hand, and powerful, rescuing divine love, on the other. The two meanings are brought into dramatic and shocking but permanent relation.[11]

People, Place, and Power in Perspective

Back in college, when I began my study on Matthew, I did not understand how all the Scriptures can and should be viewed through a kingdom lens. Part of the reason for my confusion about the kingdom was that the gospel had somehow been abstracted in my mind. I needed to be reminded of the story, hopes, and dreams of Israel. When I revisited the narrative of the Old Testament, I then understood what Jesus meant when he said that the kingdom of God was at hand. The words of Jesus bloomed as Israel's hopes for a king came into focus.

---

9. Herman Ridderbos, *The Coming Kingdom* (Phillipsburg, NJ: P&R, 1962), 169–74.

10. Treat, *The Crucified King*, 17.

11. N. T. Wright, *How God Became King: The Forgotten Story of the Gospels* (San Francisco: HarperOne, 2012), 220.

From beginning to end, the Scriptures present the story of the kingdom. If you grasp the nature of the kingdom, then the Scriptures can be seen as a coherent narrative rather than a disparate collection of stories. The fact that Adam and Eve were to be rulers over the land should inform Jesus's miracles of healing. The call of Abraham is no longer about some wandering idolater, but about the overarching story of God's concern for his people. The Wisdom Literature is no longer just a collection of proverbs, but a picture of living the good life under the ideal King. Most importantly, Jesus's mission and the gospel of the kingdom come into full clarity. When Jesus announces that the "kingdom of God" is at hand, he is announcing that in his person all the promises of God are yes and amen (see 2 Cor. 1:20).

And the promises of the kingdom are earthy. They are depicted to Abraham as land, children, and blessing (Genesis 12). In Deuteronomy they are defined as barns being full (Deut. 28:7–12). In Hosea the blessings are marked as the grain flourishing and the vine blossoming (Hos. 14:7). In Jeremiah the Lord says he will make them walk by brooks of water (Jer. 31:9), and they shall be radiant over the grain, the wine, the oil, the flock, and the herd; their life shall be like a watered garden (Jer. 31:12). In Amos the Lord promises that he will "rebuild the ruined cities and inhabit them; / they shall plant vineyards and drink their wine, / and they shall make gardens and eat their fruit" (Amos 9:14–15).

When Jesus arrives, he does not spiritualize these promises. He eats with sinners, provides food, heals people's bodies, washes the disciples' feet, and gives them his body and blood. Paul, in a similar way, instructs the kingdom citizens how to relate to one another in the tangibility of life. They are to wait and eat together, to bear one another's burdens, and share with the poor. In Revelation, the final picture is one of a city with high walls, gates, rivers, and trees.

All these are pictures of the kingdom. The kingdom is not simply social ethics, or heaven, or the church, or God's sovereignty; the kingdom is much larger. Only when we connect the dots from the first page of the Bible to the last do we begin to see that on every page the kingdom concerns the King, his people, and their place. And at the center of this kingdom plan stands a wooden cross covered in blood.

For Further Reading

Abernethy, Andrew. *The Book of Isaiah and God's Kingdom: A Thematic-Theological Approach*. Downers Grove, IL: IVP Academic, 2016.

Dempster, Stephen. *Dominion and Dynasty: A Theology of the Hebrew Bible*. New Studies in Biblical Theology. Downers Grove, IL: IVP Academic, 2003.

Goldsworthy, Graeme. *The Goldsworthy Trilogy: Gospel and Kingdom, Gospel and Wisdom, The Gospel in Revelation*. Exeter, UK: Paternoster, 2011.

Hahn, Scott. "Kingdom and Church in Luke-Acts: From Davidic Christology to Kingdom Ecclesiology." In *Reading Luke: Interpretation, Reflections, Formation*, edited by Bartholomew, Joel Green, and Anthony Thiselton, 294–326. Scripture and Hermeneutics 6. Grand Rapids, MI: Zondervan, 2005.

———. *The Kingdom of God as Liturgical Empire: A Theological Commentary on 1–2 Chronicles*. Grand Rapids, MI: Baker Academic, 2012.

Jipp, Joshua W. *Christ Is King: Paul's Royal Ideology*. Minneapolis, MN: Fortress Press, 2015.

Kupp, David. *Matthew's Emmanuel: Divine Presence and God's People in the First Gospel*. Cambridge, UK: Cambridge University Press, 1996.

Ladd, George Eldeon. *Gospel of the Kingdom: Scriptural Studies in the Kingdom of God*. Grand Rapids, MI: Eerdmans, 1959.

McCartney, Dan. "Ecce Homo: The Coming of the Kingdom as the Restoration of Human Vicegerency." *Westminster Theological Journal* 56.1 (1994): 1–21.

Merrill, Eugene H. *Everlasting Dominion: A Theology of the Old Testament*. Nashville, TN: B&H Academic, 2006.

Ridderbos, Herman. *The Coming Kingdom*. Phillipsburg, NJ: P&R, 1962.

———. *When the Time Had Fully Come: Studies in New Testament Theology*. Grand Rapids, MI: Eerdmans, 1957.

Schreiner, Thomas R. *The King in His Beauty: A Biblical Theology of the Old and New Testaments*. Grand Rapids, MI: Baker Academic, 2013.

Treat, Jeremy R. *The Crucified King: Atonement and Kingdom in Biblical and Systematic Theology*. Grand Rapids, MI: Zondervan, 2014.

Wright, N. T. *How God Became King: The Forgotten Story of the Gospels*. San Francisco: HarperOne, 2012.

General Index

Scripture Index

Short Studies in Biblical Theology Series

THE SON OF GOD
AND THE NEW CREATION

GRAEME GOLDSWORTHY

MARRIAGE
AND THE MYSTERY OF THE GOSPEL

RAY ORTLUND

WORK
AND OUR LABOR IN THE LORD

JAMES M. HAMILTON JR.

COVENANT
AND GOD'S PURPOSE FOR THE WORLD

THOMAS R. SCHREINER

THE KINGDOM OF GOD
AND THE GLORY OF THE CROSS

PATRICK SCHREINER

THE CITY OF GOD
AND THE GOAL OF CREATION

T. DESMOND ALEXANDER

For more information, visit crossway.org/ssbt.